Industrial Development in Pre-Communist China 1912-1949

Industrial Development in Pre-Communist China

1912-1949

John K. Chang

Routledge
Taylor & Francis Group

LONDON AND NEW YORK

Originally published in 1969 by Edinburgh University Press.

Published 2010 by Transaction Publishers

Published 2017 by Routledge
2 Park Square, Milton Park, Abingdon, Oxon OX14 4RN
711 Third Avenue, New York, NY 10017, USA

Routledge is an imprint of the Taylor & Francis Group, an informa business

Library of Congress Catalog Number: 2010003970

Library of Congress Cataloging-in-Publication Data

Chang, John K. (John Key), 1933-
  Industrial development in pre-communist China : 1912-1949 / John K. Chang.
        p. cm.
  Includes bibliographical references and index.
  Commissioned by the Committee on the Economy of China of the Social Science Research Council.
  Reprint. Originally published: Edinburgh University Press, 1969.
  ISBN 978-0-202-36366-0 (alk. paper)
  1. Industries--China. 2. Industrialization--China. I. Social Science Research Council (U.S.). Committee on the Economy of China. II. Title.

HC427.8 .C448
338.095109'041--dc22
                                                          2010003970
ISBN 13: 978-0-202-36366-0 (pbk)

Foreword

The record of industrial development in China under the Communists has been the subject of intense scrutiny. What is revealed is that after an initial period of reconstruction, the rate of industrial growth was exceedingly rapid until the advent of the Great Leap Forward. What happened afterward is still not entirely clear, but it is the consensus of Western scholars that industry was well on the road to recovery after a deep depression only to be set back once again by the Cultural Revolution.

In contrast to the well-studied decades since 1949, surprisingly little attention has been paid to the pre-Communist industrial history of China. The absence of thoroughgoing quantitative analysis, in particular, has led to the belief that the condition of the vast Chinese mainland before the Communist takeover is best described as one of economic stagnation. It is to an examination of this proposition that the present work is addressed.

Professor Chang has constructed an index of industrial production for China for the period 1912 to 1949, based upon a good deal of statistical information. It appears from his data that for the period as a whole, industry grew at the quite respectable rate of 5.6 per cent per annum. If one abstracts from the cataclysmic military events that befell China, the record is even more impressive. From 1912 to 1936, the latter year marking the peak of the pre-Sino-Japanese War era, the industrial growth rate was 9.4 per cent annually. And even if one leaves aside the unusual estimates provided by World War I and its aftermath, the growth rate (1923 to 1936) is still 8.7 per cent.

What Professor Chang has established beyond doubt is that China managed to attain a substantial expansion of its modern industrial sector before the Japanese invasion. This might well have led to self-sustaining growth if relatively peaceful conditions had continued to prevail. While the Communist industrial achievement during the first Five-Year Plan should not be denigrated, the fact that there was a successful precedent helps place that achievement in its proper perspective.

This study is the product of a project commissioned by the Committee on the Economy of China of the Social Science Research Council, supported by a grant from the Ford Foundation. The Committee endeavors to insure that its projects will be conducted with scholarly objectivity and accuracy, in furtherance of its mandate to stimulate scientific analysis of the contemporary scene on the Chinese mainland. Final responsibility and full credit for the finished work, however, must remain with the author.

WALTER GALENSON

Acknowledgments

Many libraries extended extraordinary privileges to me in the course of this study. Among them, special mention should be made of the Harvard-Yenching Library, the Hoover Library at Stanford University, the Chinese and Japanese Sections of the U.S. Library of Congress, the Asia Library of the University of Michigan, the Oriental Collection in the National Agricultural Library of the U.S. Department of Agriculture, the National Diet Library of Japan, the Library of the Department of Economics at Kyoto University, the Library of the Institute of Economics at Hitotsubashi University, and the Toyo Bunko Collection in Tokyo.

During a visit to Taiwan, I interviewed and consulted with leading experts in universities, government, and industries; Mr. Lu Hsien-chi of the Ministry of Economic Affairs in Taipei arranged some of these meetings. In Taiwan, Hsing Mo-huan, Director of the Institute of Economic Research of Academia Sinica, and Ch'uan Han-sheng, Professor of Economic History at National Taiwan University, gave me much encouragement and guidance.

Dr. Fred C. Hung of the University of Hawaii made available for my unlimited use his personal research files and data collection on China's industrial development. His unreserved generosity requires much more than a formal acknowledgment here.

Many other scholars, too, have helped to bring this volume to completion. Among them, Robert F. Dernberger and Albert Feuerwerker of the University of Michigan, Franklin

L. Ho of Columbia University, Hou Chi-ming of Colgate University, Ishikawa Shigeru of Hitotsubashi University, and Simon Kuznets and Dwight H. Perkins of Harvard University read the manuscript at various stages and made many helpful suggestions. Rockwood Chin of the University of Connecticut made valuable comments on my cotton yarn and cloth estimates. Chao Kang of the University of Wisconsin helped me in the formative stages of this study. Cheng Chu-yuan of the University of Michigan and Wan Wei-ying of Yale University (then at the University of Michigan) enlightened me on a number of important background issues over countless cups of coffee. Arthur N. Young, financial adviser to the Chinese Government during 1929–1947, made extremely detailed comments on the entire manuscript. My colleagues at Lafayette provided friendly and stimulating surroundings. Walter Galenson, Director of Research of this monograph series, read the manuscript several times and made significant contributions to the improvement of the manuscript between drafts. Finally, to Alexander Eckstein, for his constant encouragement and enlightenment from the beginning of the study to its final stage of publication, I owe the greatest debt of all. He read the various drafts of the manuscript with extreme care, asked searching questions, uncovered a number of shortcomings, and shared his insights with me. I hope that the book in its present form will please him and others, for on the whole I accepted their advice.

The Center for Chinese Studies of the University of Michigan, provided financial support which enabled me to begin the research for this study. The Committee on the Economy of China of the Social Science Research Council, furnished grants which made possible the completion of the volume. Lafayette College granted me a partial leave of absence during the Spring semester of 1967 which enabled me to begin the first draft.

I also appreciate the help of Mrs. Winifred Brown, Mrs. Catherine Poch, and Mrs. Mary Ann Serio in typing and preparing the manuscript for publication. Mrs. Shirley Clarkson greatly improved the book's style and readability. Finally, without the patience, sacrifice, and wholehearted support of my wife, even this small volume would not have been possible. In the course of this study I took much away from her and the children that was rightfully theirs.

JOHN K. CHANG

Contents

List of Tables and Charts

*Industrial
Development in
Pre-Communist
China*

CHAPTER ONE

Introduction

PURPOSE

THE ECONOMY OF Communist China has been, in recent years, the subject of much research in the United States and abroad. Most of the studies have been preoccupied with measuring economic growth and development, in the aggregate and for major sectors of the economy and particular industries. Among these studies are general surveys of the Chinese economy and quantitative assessments of Communist China's national income and industrial production. However, notably lacking have been studies of the rate and extent of growth of China's agriculture.

There have been, of course, studies on Communist China's economic systems and institutions. Their general orientation has gradually shifted away from simple fact-finding to a more rigorous analysis of the performance of the Chinese economy and a critical assessment of the functioning of China's economic systems and institutions.[1] These studies have

1. One example of this shift in research orientation is shown by Dwight H. Perkins, 1966.

enhanced our understanding of the Chinese economy and illuminated many problems. However, a major shortcoming has been their relatively scanty reference to the economic past. Perhaps giving priority to the study of recent developments has made this shortcoming inevitable. Nevertheless, whatever the cause, it is not possible to make accurate observations or to draw conclusions about the economic growth and industrial development of Mainland China under the Communist regime based only on post-1949 events.

An economic historian, looking at a particular country's economic growth experience, often seeks to identify the long-term continuity or discontinuity of historical events. Discontinuities are usually obvious and perhaps sometimes overemphasized, while continuities are frequently hidden and difficult to discover. The rapid economic expansion and the successful economic transformation of Meiji Japan, for example, must be analyzed in the context of historical events, particularly economic developments, of the Tokugawa period. The economic development of Meiji Japan would probably be incomprehensible without such a historical perspective.[2] For the same reasons, the economic developments of Communist China should be appraised in the light of economic events of the Republican (1912–49) and even the pre-Republican periods.

While there has been very little reference made to the economic past in most of the economic studies on Communist China, several writers in this field have attempted, with varying degrees of success, to link the present with the past.[3]

2. See, for example, Lockwood and Crawcour in William W. Lockwood, 1965 (pp. 3–5, 17–44).
3. See, for example, Cheng Chu-yuan, 1963, particularly the chapter, "China's Pre-Communist Economic Structure"; Alexander Eckstein, 1966 (ch. 2); Albert Feuerwerker, 1964; Liu Ta-chung and Yeh Kung-chia, 1965 (ch. 1, esp. pp. 3–4); and Wu Yuan-li, 1965 (esp. pp. 124–29).

These attempts are still of a pioneering nature, but they do show the importance of knowing in what ways and to what extent China's economic heritage is responsible for the economic developments of the present period. Unfortunately, the existing knowledge of the past does not permit exact statements.

One common notion, among specialists and laymen alike, about the economic growth and industrial development of pre-Communist Mainland China is that it was characterized by long-term stagnation, and that China on the eve of the Communist take-over had little or no industrial base.[4] Another view contends that there were periods of rapid industrial growth in the pre-Communist period, and that a fairly sizable industrial base was developed, at least in Manchuria and the treaty ports.[5]

It is the purpose of this study to build a reasonably accurate and comprehensive record of China's industrial development during the pre-Communist period. Such a long-term record of rates and levels of industrial output not only may enable us to learn and study the lessons of the past, but also may serve as a useful historical base against which to appraise the economic achievements of the Communist regime in recent years.

INDUSTRIAL DEVELOPMENT IN CHINA BEFORE 1912

Descriptive information on the state of the Chinese economy before 1912 in general and industrial development in

4. For nineteenth-century China, see John K. Fairbank, Alexander Eckstein, and L. S. Yang, 1960 (pp. 1–26) and Dwight H. Perkins, 1967 (pp. 478–92). For the Nanking period, see Douglas S. Paauw, 1957 (pp. 213–20).
5. Hou Chi-ming (1965, pp. 125–27), for example, shows that, in quantitative terms, the modern sector of the Chinese economy expanded continuously and at a constant rate from the 1860's to the 1930's.

particular are relatively plentiful, but quantitative data, especially long-term time series, are extremely scarce and scattered. For this reason, it has been found impossible to make quantitative measurements of industrial development prior to 1912. However, before proceeding to a detailed analysis of the period from 1912 to 1949, it seems desirable to give a brief view of the pre-1912 period.

Several economic historians have dated the genesis of China's industrialization as far back as 1862, but it has been generally agreed that modern industrial development on any significant scale did not take place until World War I.[6] Some writers have tried to divide the period between 1862 and 1911 so as to identify and analyze the changing characteristics of China's industrialization. Different opinions have resulted from these periodization attempts. Kung Chün (1933, pp. 13–14, 49–50, 65–69), for example, divides this span into four periods:[7] (1) 1862 to 1877 was a period of military oriented industrialization, characterized by ammunition manufacturing. In an effort to improve and fortify China's defense capability by adopting Western-style military and technological know-how, such leaders as Tseng Kuo-fang and Li Hung-chang promoted the establishment of arsenals and shipyards for the production of military equipment. (2) From 1878 to 1894, the so-called *Kuan-tu shang-pan* type of enterprise developed and flourished. This system was characterized by government supervision or sponsorship of private (commercial and industrial) enterprises. (According to Albert Feuerwerker [1958, p. 9], this form of organization was most widespread during the period, although other forms were also found. Nevertheless, there were only a few

---

6. See, for example, Kung Chün, 1933; Yang Ch'üan, 1923; and Yang Ta-chin, 1928 (Vol. 1, pp. 1–29).

7. A number of other writers on this topic either followed or modified Kung's periodization, which seems to be considered as the standard.

large enterprises organized during this period that could really be classified as *Kuan-tu shang-pan* establishments.[8]) (3) The period from 1895 to 1902 was marked by the beginning of foreign economic penetration and, in some cases, the domination of China. Japan was granted the privilege of establishing industrial and commercial enterprises in the treaty ports under the provisions of the Treaty of Shimonoseki, and other powers shared this privilege through the most-favored-nation clause. As a result, foreign enterprises made large-scale investment in China. (4) The period from 1903 to 1911 saw a transition from the *Kuan-tu shang-pan* system to completely privately owned and managed enterprises. The role of government during this period was limited to promoting and encouraging industrialization efforts, and, on the whole, the public response was positive. (See Perkins, 1967.)

Statistical data on industrial development for the pre-1912 period are fragmentary, and the quality of such data is far from satisfactory. For example, in 1912, according to one source (Nung-shang-pu, 1922, p. 261), there were 20,749 so-called "factories" in China, employing a total of 661,784 workers, with an average of about 32 workers per "factory."[9] "Factory" as used in this source is any small workshop employing 7 or more workers. Neither the degree of capitalization nor the method of production were taken into consideration in defining "factory." Among the 20,749 "factories" reported, only 363 used mechanical power. In other words, only about 1.7 per cent of the "factories" were mechanized. Moreover, it has been estimated that there were only 737 pieces of

8. Feuerwerker's book is a study of the economic condition of the late Ch'ing period, and a study of the *Kuan-tu shang-pan* system in particular.

9. In some industries the average number of employees per establishment was considerably larger. In 1912, the average number of employees per cotton spinning and weaving establishment, for example, was 1,122; in silk reeling, 296; in tea processing, 236; and in matches and gunpowder, 131 (Nung-shang-pu, 1922, pp. 265–66).

mechanized equipment, using steam, electric, or other power in these 363 "mechanized factories" (Nung-shang-pu, 1922, p. 261)—on an average, only about 2 pieces of mechanized equipment per "mechanized factory." The low degree of mechanization in Chinese industries in 1912 needs no further demonstration. Other available data,[10] less adequate, indicate that most of the industrial and commercial establishments in pre-1912 China had limited capital resources and were concentrated in Shanghai and other treaty ports.

These were the general trends of industrial development prior to 1912, as indicated by available data. By 1912, China's industrialization efforts had resulted in several large-scale establishments with a high degree of capitalization and mechanization, such as the Hanyehping Coal and Iron Corporation. However, these efforts were not accompanied by the development of the necessary infrastructure or by sweeping reforms for modernization. For this reason, China's industrialization did not result in any evident structural changes in the economy (cf. Kuznets, 1966, p. 475).

<h2 style="text-align:center">TIME PERIOD</h2>

For lack of adequate statistical information, the initial year for this study could not go back to 1862 or even to 1895. The reason for beginning this analysis with 1912 is not influenced by political factors. Rather, as has been indicated, 1912 seems to be the earliest year for which relatively systematic long-term industrial information, at least for mining products, becomes available.

From 1912 to 1949, the period chosen for the study, China experienced a number of violent disturbances, both internal and external. As we shall see, they had damaging effects on the

10. Statistical tables published by the Nung-kung-shang-pu (The Ministry of Agriculture, Industry, and Commerce) in 1909 and 1910. For a partial summary of these tables, see Yen Chung-p'ing *et al.*, 1955 (pp. 93–99).

Chinese economy and a crippling impact on China's efforts to industrialize.

Despite the founding of the Republic of China with its republican form of central government, the country was still far from political unity and stability. Much of the country was in the hands of military leaders who had effective control of semi-autonomous regions.[11] For some time the central constitutional government was not only powerless but actually in peril. It was not until 1928, at the successful conclusion of the Northern Expedition, that the country was finally unified politically, at least temporarily, under the Nanking Government. Only then did the government have a breathing spell and begin to direct its attention to socioeconomic problems and to measures for industrialization.[12] A number of important economic measures were put into effect in the brief period between 1928 and the early 1930's.

Just as the government and its people began to look forward to a brighter future, there came the surprise attack of the Japanese in Manchuria in September, 1931, and the Japanese naval invasion of Shanghai in January, 1932. This changed the outlook completely. The Sino-Japanese War finally came in 1937, and lasted until 1945. The material loss and the crippling effect on the Chinese economy were great, with industrial output declining drastically from 1936 to 1937. For example, in Shanghai the output of cotton textile industries fell by 35 per cent. Other industries experienced a similar decline during this period. (See Economic Research Bureau of Shanghai,

11. Yen Hsi-shan, for example, dominated not only the politics but also the industry and commerce of Shansi and the neighboring Suiyaun province from about 1916 to 1949. (See Donald G. Gillin, 1967.)

12. Small-scale revolts and political unrest continued to be the order of the day. Feng Yu-hsiang, for example, revolted in Honan in May, 1929; Tang Shen-chih in December, 1929, in Hunan; Yen Hsi-shan in 1930; Feng again in May, 1933, in Kalgan; Chen Chi-tang in 1936; and so on. Meanwhile, party disunity resulted in the stepping-down of Generalissimo Chiang Kai-shek in December, 1931, and the reorganization of the National Government.

1945, p. 194; Central Bank of China, 1948, p. 22.) Industries in the southwestern hinterland were developed by the government after 1938, but this was limited in scope. Manchuria, on the other hand, continued to develop during the war because of the vigorous efforts of the Japanese. The larger part of China remained in a crippled condition throughout the war years. With the end of war in 1945, the National Government only had time to shift the direction of its military efforts, this time against the Chinese Communists.[13] Finally, in 1949, the government was evacuated to Taiwan.

Despite the difficulties of obtaining data for the war years, the entire Republican period is considered in this study, since one of our primary tasks is to set the record of industrial development straight, to find out, as fully as possible and in quantitative terms, what has actually happened. Such a long-term record of industrial performance of China, if established reasonably accurately, is useful not only in and of itself but is also an indispensable historical basis for appraising Communist China's economic development.

METHODOLOGY AND SCOPE

One approach to the task of building a long-term historical record of industrial development is to construct an overall index of industrial production for the pre-Communist period. A number of indexes of industrial production have been constructed during the past few decades by scholars both in the United States and in China. These are inadequate and incomplete in the sense that they cover only a few key commodities series, a short span of time, or a limited geographical region. None of these is strictly comparable with the ones attempted in this study.

13. The Japanese surrendered on August 14, 1945, and the fighting against the Chinese Communists resumed on October 28, 1945.

Fred C. Hung (1958), for example, has constructed an index for six major commodities from 1922 to 1936. In China, several industrial production indexes were constructed. Wang Foh-shen, a principal collaborator of Ou Pao-san, compiled an index covering eleven commodities for the period 1931–1946, for the whole country (1948a). Wang also constructed separate wartime industrial production indexes for North China and Free China (1948b). The Central Bank of China compiled an index for the early 1930's. The Department of Statistics of the Ministry of Economic Affairs published output indexes for a wide range of industrial commodities, but this was confined to the then "Free-China." Some of these indexes will be presented and discussed in detail in chapter 4 and will be compared with the results of this study.

One purpose here is to construct a more comprehensive index of industrial production, both in terms of time span and product coverage. For purposes of this study, "industrial production" includes the following output categories: mining, metallurgy, manufacturing, fuel, and power. Construction is excluded.[14] Moreover, the study is more or less confined to the output of factory industry. The output of the handicraft sector will be analyzed, but a long-term output index including handicrafts is impossible because of inadequate data.

In combining the individual output series, a simple index-number formula has been used.[15] In algebraic terms, the formula is expressed as follows:

$$\frac{\sum p_0 q_1}{\sum p_0 q_0}$$

14. Cf. the international standard industrial classification of all economic activities, which includes construction activities. A list of the commodity series included in the indexes will be found in chapter 2.

15. Much attention has been given in the literature to the so-called "ideal" index of industrial output which is supposed to measure the movements of total value of net output resulting from changes in the physical quantities of

The subscripts 0 and 1 denote the two time periods compared; p represents the set of prices or weights selected for weighting the physical quantities, q_0 and q_1, compared. The p coefficient selected is in value terms, and both gross price and value-added weights have been used in this study. The resulting index, using value-added as weights, is not a precise measurement of net output, but it should reflect the changes in the levels of net output.

More specifically, the value-added weights used in this study are net value-added per unit of product, that is, the gross value of products minus cost of materials and fuel consumed, less depreciation allowances, per unit of product. These value-added data, however, are not completely free of duplication, because certain business service expenses, such as advertising and insurance, are included. As long as business service costs are not proportionately distributed among the industries, their inclusion would distort the relative importance of the industries included in the index. The problem is not serious in the case of China, since such costs represent only a negligible fraction of the total cost of production.

Guided by data limitations, we constructed only one index using 1933 net value-added weights. This index is compared with one weighted by 1933 gross prices. Another set of indexes

---

final products and from changes in the physical quantities of material consumed in the production process of those final products, both the products produced and the materials consumed are valued at fixed prices. In symbolical terms, the formula will take the following form:

$$\frac{\Sigma p_0 q_1 - P_0 Q_1}{\Sigma p_0 q_0 - P_0 Q_0}$$

where the small letters denote the quantity and price of final products and the capital letters those of raw materials. There is no denying that this elaborate formula excels the others with respect to its measurement of net industrial output. But in order to use it in computing the indexes of output an extensive set of raw data would be necessary. Of related interest, cf. Boris P. Pesek, 1961 (pp. 295–315).

weighted by 1925, 1933, and 1952 gross prices, respectively, are presented in Appendix C for comparative purposes. The interpretative analysis, found in chapters 5 and 6, has relied almost exclusively upon the index using 1933 net value-added weights.

An attempt has been made to cover all of China irrespective of changes in political boundaries. Following this guideline, Manchuria was not excluded between 1931–1945. By the same token, the other Japanese-occupied areas of China during the Sino-Japanese conflict were included, although the coverage is poor for lack of adequate data.

In the chapters that follow, we consider first the most formidable difficulty encountered in this study: the absence or scarcity of reliable and comprehensive output statistics. The availability and reliability of the data will be discussed in chapter 2 and in the appendixes. Chapter 2 contains a series of qualifying remarks applicable to all the statistical and interpretative analyses that follow. Chapter 3 will be devoted to a discussion of the problem of coverage and to a survey of the industries not covered in this study.

The statistical results of the study will be presented in chapter 4, along with those of other scholars who have made similar but not strictly comparable attempts. Finally, in chapters 5 and 6, some observations and interpretative analyses of China's industrialization will be made, primarily on the basis of the 1933 net value-added index.

The scope of this study is limited. It is primarily exploratory in nature and quantitative in approach. It will not discuss many of the important noneconomic issues and events of the period, except where such discussion is needed to make the analysis more intelligible. However, this represents at least a preliminary step toward a more comprehensive and quantitative study of the history of China's industrialization. Finally, this study is directed toward the ultimate goal of understanding more fully and interpreting more accurately the contemporary economic development of Communist China and eventually the historical development of the Chinese economy in the twentieth century.

CHAPTER TWO

The Data

THE QUALITY AND usefulness of an index of industrial production depends upon the raw data used and the methodology followed. Even with data of high quality, the use of a biased formula or of improper weights would render the index meaningless. More importantly, if the quality of raw data is poor, no methodology, however refined, could produce an index of better quality than that of the basic materials. This chapter discusses the availability and quality of the basic production and other related statistics used. The 15 production series included in the indexes cover a reasonably high percentage of total industrial output and possess a high degree of representativeness, but the gaps and discontinuities in the long-term compilation of data are numerous and serious. Different methods of estimation, depending upon the nature of cases concerned, have been used to fill the gaps. It is only proper to bring these to the attention of the reader, so that he may be in a better position to evaluate the observations and conclusions drawn on the basis of these indexes.

The compiled as well as the estimated data, with accompanying explanatory notes and detailed source references, are presented in the appendixes. In chapter 3 we shall survey the growth and development of the industries omitted in this study and consider the extent and direction of the effects of the indexes of such omissions.

INDUSTRIAL STATISTICS OF CHINA

Even a brief survey of the literature indicates that relatively abundant and comprehensive industrial statistics are available only for the first half of the 1930's. Before and after this period, industrial statistics were not compiled systematically for the nation as a whole either by governmental or by private agencies. It is impossible, therefore, to compile long-term production data or any other industrial statistics on China from the relatively few high-quality official and nonofficial sources, even for the principal commodities, *e.g.,* cotton yarn and flour. Consequently, compilation of almost all of the long-term series required a search of all possible sources, including yearbooks, government documents and other publications, books and monographs, journal articles, and so on.

As early as 1912, the Ministry of Agriculture and Commerce (Nung-shang-pu) of the Peking Government conducted an overall survey of China's agriculture and industries. This survey compiled and reported annually statistical information on agricultural and industrial production, the number of "factories" (meaning workshops employing seven or more workers), employment, capacity and so on. This report and each subsequent annual issue represented fairly closely a census of manufacture, although it did not cover as many industries or industrial commodities as one would have wished (Nung-shang-pu, 1914–24).

The quality of these reports leaves much to be desired. Not only is the coverage of commodities incomplete, but after 1915, probably due to continuous civil strife, the number of local authorities submitting economic data to the Peking Government diminished year by year. By 1921, in the tenth and final annual report, only ten provinces were included, and the usefulness of the report as a source of information became highly limited. In fact, only the first four reports (1912 to 1915) have reasonably good coverage.

Even for the early years, reporting was inaccurate and imprecise. This can be attributed to inexperience in data compilation and partly to lack of proper care in reporting and printing. Moreover, there were numerous obvious errors in the annual reports. Some of the reported figures simply cannot be substantiated. For example, cotton cloth production was about three million bolts in 1925, as reported by the Chinese Cotton Millowners' Association, a most reliable source for Chinese cotton textile data. (See Yen Chung-p'ing *et al.*, 1955, p. 130.) But the annual reports for 1912–15 reported outputs of cotton cloth several times greater than the 1925 production. (Nung-shang-pu, No. 7, pp. 340–41). Granted that these output figures included cloth production by the handlooms, a separation by methods of production should have been made.

Apparently, there were several typographical errors which remained uncorrected issue after issue, indicating carelessness and negligence on the part of the statistical compilers. In view of these problems, it has been decided not to use here the statistical information contained in these reports, despite the fact that they are probably the only comprehensive and centralized source of economic statistics for the first few years of the Republican period.

In 1927, when the National Government was established in Nanking, a number of government agencies, recognizing

the need for statistical information, began to compile indu
trial statistics in a more comprehensive and systematic manner
These efforts resulted in a large number of publications,
handbooks, and journals appearing during the early 1930's.
By this time, the groundwork of statistical data compilatic
for China was fairly well laid. In 1930, the Ministry of Industr
Commerce, and Labor (Kung-shang-pu) of the Nation
Government conducted regional and local surveys of indu
tries which covered the major provinces and cities. Similar
surveys were carried out annually beginning in 1933 by the
Ministry of Industries (Shih-yeh-pu). Among the statistics
compiled, major categories included the number of factories,
the amount of capital, employment, wages, capacity, and raw
materials consumed.

In addition to the above, an outstanding example of the
government's strong interest in the compilation of industrial
statistics was the completion of a national survey of Chinese-
owned modern industries. In 1933, D. K. Lieu, Director of the
China Institute of Economic and Statistical Research of
Shanghai, undertook the survey, at the request of the National
Resources Commission of the National Government. The
results were published in three volumes in 1937, complete with
tables and statistics. It was the first and remains the only
comprehensive industrial census China has ever produced.
Under the direction and supervision of D. K. Lieu, a group of
well-trained investigators surveyed almost all of China
(excluding Manchuria), covering a total of 17 provinces and
4 major industrial centers (Shanghai, Nanking, Peiping and
Tsingtao). Detailed information on the gross value and quantity of output, employment, materials and fuel consumed, and
other industrial statistics in 16 manufacturing industries were
included in the survey. The survey was conducted only for one
year, 1933, and much of the information reported was actually
for the year 1932. The survey, confined to the Chinese-owned

factories employing 30 or more workers and using mechanical power, left a substantial portion of China's industrial activities uncovered. Other studies have subsequently filled some of these gaps.

These government efforts and genuine interest in industrial data compilation came to a halt when the war broke out in 1937 but resumed almost immediately and continued throughout the war years. However, data compilation covered only those limited areas under government control. The system and technique of data compilation was considerably improved during the war years, and the Bureau of Statistics of the Ministry of Economic Affairs (Ching-chi-pu t'ung-chi-ch'u) of the National Government in Chungking systematically collected and published a series of industrial and mining statistics (Ching-chi-pu, 1944, 1945).

A number of private trade associations and research organizations also made valuable contributions in building China's statistical information system. The Chinese Cotton Millowners' Association compiled thorough mill statistics, including output, spindleage and loomage, employment, etc., throughout the 1920's and the early 1930's. This, too, was ended by the outbreak of war in 1937. D. K. Lieu's China Institute of Economic and Statistical Research made industrial surveys of Shanghai. The Economic Research Institute of Nankai University, under the leadership of a number of well-trained economists, thoroughly surveyed the Tientsin area and parts of North China. Some of the provincial and municipal governments also made regional studies and surveys from time to time.

Statistics of mining in China are relatively complete and abundant. Beginning in 1912, the Peking Government compiled and reported some mining statistics in its annual statistical tables, but, as noted earlier, this source is of questionable reliability. The major effort in conducting geological surveys and collecting mineral output data was made by the Geological Survey of China (Ti-chih tiao-ch'a-so) of the National Government, under the leadership of a number of prominent and dedicated scholars and geologists, including the famed Wong Wen-hao. The work of this particular organization does not seem to have been much affected by the outbreak of military hostilities. On the contrary, data compilation and reporting continued, progressed, and was evidently improved. In the seven issues of *The General Statement on the Mining Industry* (*Chung-kuo k'uang-yeh chi-yao*), published simultaneously in Chinese and English over a period of 24 years (between 1921 and 1945), data on output for most mineral products, covering both China proper and Manchuria, are available from 1912 to 1942. Given its leadership and long history in data compilation, the statistical information supplied by the Geological Survey of China should be fairly reliable and of high quality.[1]

Data on Manchurian industries are not as readily available, as one would expect. It is true that the South Manchuria Railway Company conducted painstaking surveys of the area and published its findings in literally thousands of volumes of documented materials. The Manchoukuo Government also undertook this work, but there was an almost complete blackout of industrial statistics when the war broke out. Output statistics were apparently considered military secrets and withheld by the authorities. This was true not only of statistics on the output of iron and steel and other strategic materials, but also of consumer goods. Even today, more than 20 years later, many of these information gaps are left unfilled. This is shown in the recent monumental work on the 40-year history of Manchuria's development (Manshikai, 1964). Gaps in output statistics are surprisingly numerous in this study, and

1. For an article on the availability of industrial statistics in China, see Chao Chang-fu, April 1943 (pp. 271–75).

it is not clear whether or not such information is obtainable.

In addition to the above-mentioned source materials, there are many books and monographs representing the results of individual research. Some of them are cited in this study and listed in the References.

OUTPUT SERIES

The data collected for this study include literally every available production figure. The number of commodities for which there is at least one output figure over the 37-year period is large indeed. At a later stage of data-gathering efforts were concentrated on some of the more promising series, that is, ones for which a reasonably complete production record might be obtained over the entire 37-year period. Thirty-three commodities were included in this category. In the final screening, only 15 series were selected for inclusion in the indexes. Most of the series were omitted because they were incomplete and discontinuous, and no reasonable method could be found to fill the gaps. Not even the 15 series included in the indexes were continuous and complete, but methodologically consistent and defensible ways have been found to estimate the gaps.

The 15 commodity series included in the indexes fall into three major industrial categories: (1) mining and metallurgy—coal, iron ore, pig iron, steel, antimony, copper, gold, mercury, tin, and tungsten; (2) manufacturing—cotton yarn, cotton cloth, and cement; and (3) fuel and power—crude oil and electric power.

Two detailed tables in Appendix A have been prepared for the convenience of those interested in raw data as well as source references. Table A–1 of Appendix A contains the output data actually collected from various sources, and

Table A–2 is a tabulation of the estimates made. A glance at the appendix will probably elicit at least two immediate reactions. First, the 15 series may seem to provide much too limited a coverage for an index of industrial production. Second, the extent to which the gaps in the series had to be filled by estimates may seem considerable. While it is true that the series leave a large area of industrial production unaccounted for, they represent a fairly complete, if not exhaustive, search and compilation of the long-term production data available, at least to scholars outside of Mainland China.

Even the reported output figures are not without defects. In the first place, output figures in a number of the series are estimates made either by the reporting agency or by individual experts, rather than by census enumerations. Take, for example, the output statistics for cotton yarn and cloth. The only authoritative and reliable data-gathering and -reporting agency was the Chinese Cotton Millowners' Association. Before the Association began compiling and reporting mill statistics in 1925, practically all cotton yarn output figures found in the literature were estimates of individual experts. Moreover, these apparently independent estimates were made by various methods, using different assumptions. As a result, one finds widely divergent cotton yarn output figures given for certain years and it is difficult to choose one estimate out of many on the basis of reliability. Furthermore, the reporting agency often fails to indicate whether or not the reported figures are estimates. In the case of cotton cloth, one hardly finds in the literature even estimated output figures before 1925.

Second, many of the reported output statistics lack descriptive details. Once again, the case of cotton textile statistics illustrates the problem. Cotton yarn output is usually reported in number of bales. It is seldom clear whether a given number of bales produced is the summation of all yarns of different counts or the converted equivalent of a particular count. The problem is more serious in the case of cloth, where the unit of measurement is usually in bolts of 40 yards. These bolts could differ substantially in width and in weight, reflecting different kinds and quality of cloth. This problem was partially solved in later years when the output was measured in square yards.

Third, geographical coverage changes over time, and such changes are often not explicitly noted by the reporting agency. Over this period of 37 years, the territory under the control of the National Government underwent drastic changes, especially during the Sino-Japanese war. In this study an effort has been made to cover China in its entirety, irrespective of its political boundaries. For the years before 1937, there is relatively little difficulty in arriving at national totals. It was only necessary to adjust for Manchurian output in certain cases. Prior to the founding of Manchoukuo, virtually all principal sources reported national figures covering both China proper and Manchuria, and no coverage adjustment was necessary. After 1937, the Japanese-occupied area of China proper varied in size from year to year and presented a serious coverage-adjustment problem. This area had virtually no reporting system, so that the output data for these regions are scanty and unreliable. Every effort was made to include this area by piecing together fragmentary and scattered information. The output data used in the indexes do include the occupied areas, at least for the major commodities.

In view of these problems, extreme care was exercised in selecting and compiling data. Whenever possible, the reported output figures, especially those where the quality is known to be questionable, were checked against other indicators for reliability and consistency. In some cases, one was fortunate enough to find only a single source of information. In most other cases, there were many divergent figures, and choice depended on which figure came from a relatively more authoritative source, was published at a more recent date, and/or checked more reasonably with other indicators. As a matter of general policy, only usable data are included, and that is why only 15 series were selected for the indexes.

Among the 15 series included in the indexes, some series are more reliable than others. Within a single series, data for certain time periods are better than for other periods. In some cases, where the national total is an aggregate of regional subtotals, the quality of data also differs from region to region. We shall now discuss some of these qualitative differences among the series.

On the whole, the series on mineral and metallurgical products are not only more complete but also more reliable than the others. Table A–1 of Appendix A indicates that these series have relatively few gaps. The gaps in coal, iron ore, and pig iron have been filled by estimates made by consistent methods. Therefore, this is a relatively complete record of production for these commodities over the entire 37-year period. The two principal sources of data for these series are: (1) the selected statistics on the economic history of modern China, edited by Yen Chung-p'ing and others; and (2) the reports by the Geological Survey of China. Both sources can be regarded as authoritative and reliable.

Some of the series on mining and metallurgy do require a word of explanation. The one on steel, for example, would appear to be strange, if not nonsensical, without a brief account of the development of the industry. There are three sudden changes in the level of output—in 1912–13, 1921–22, and 1934–35. Prior to 1917, the Hanyehping Coal and Iron Company, consisting of the Hanyang Iron Works, the Tayeh Iron Mines, and the P'inghsiang Coal Mines was the sole producer of steel in China. The first sudden jump in output reflects the rapid recovery made by the company from a crisis precipitated by the political-military turmoil of the country, and by the financial-administrative difficulties of the company at the time of the 1911 Revolution. The recorded increase in output from 1912 to 1913 was found although not explained in all published works on the company's history, and there is no reason to question its authenticity.

In 1922 the company's Hanyang plant was shut down completely, and steel production at that plant came to a halt. This is reflected in the sudden drop in output from 1921 to 1922. Beginning in 1935, because of Japanese efforts, plants in Manchuria, principally at Anshan and Penchihu, stepped up their production. This resulted in rapid advances for the industry until the peak was reached in 1943.[2]

The principal source of data for the steel series used in this study is Yen Chung-p'ing's *Selected Statistics* (1955). For the period 1922–34, the output figures are in round numbers. They are apparently only rough estimates of output of the smaller plants. The same set of rough estimates has been found in almost every other source. It is not clear why more accurate output figures were not available for this particular period.

Of lesser importance is the copper series, for which output data were extremely difficult to find, especially for the early years. For the years from 1912 to 1924, no reliable national data were found, and the figures recorded in the series are only the aggregate output of the principal producing regions. Copper output was so small that even a wide margin of error in the output data could not produce serious distortion, since the series would have only small weight in the composite index. The compilation of the remaining mining series was fairly routine and requires no explanation.

2. For a descriptive account of the industry, see Chang Tzu-k'ai, 1954 (Vol. I, pp. 1–58). For an account of the Hanyehping Company in particular, see, for example, Albert Feuerwerker, in C. D. Cowan, 1964 (pp. 79–110).

The five remaining series are of inferior quality as compared to the above ten. The cotton yarn data are relatively complete and continuous, but data for many of the early years consist of estimates representing the research results of a number of experts. The margin of error in each case is not easily ascertainable. For the war years, 1937–45, cotton yarn data were either unavailable or inadequate. In some cases there was no complete regional information for deriving national totals. But in these cases, as a minimum, the aggregate output of Free and North China, Manchuria, and Shanghai was calculated to represent the national totals. The margin of error resulting from the omission of regional subtotals is not likely to be substantial for any of the war years, since none of the uncovered areas (mainly the Japanese-occupied areas exclusive of Manchuria and North China) had been a cotton yarn producing center before the war or was likely to become one during the war. Moreover, these uncovered regions remained largely in a crippled condition and could not have been making any significant contribution to industrial production during the war years.

The cotton cloth data are much less complete than the cotton yarn data. It was necessary to make output estimates for the long period, 1912–26, and for other years as well. For details of the method of estimation used, the reader is referred to the next section in this chapter.

The cement series is comparatively good, since output data for most years are fairly complete. However, two possible sources of error should be pointed out. For the period 1912–21, no output figures were found for the nation as a whole. This part of the cement series represents the output of only two principal cement companies: the Chinese-owned Ch'i-hsin and the Dairen Branch of the Japanese Onoda. Evidence shows that for the early years the combined output of these two companies probably accounted for a substantial portion of the cement produced in China.[3] Second, between 1932 and 1945, regional outputs were aggregated to derive the national totals. Some Japanese-occupied areas had to be omitted for lack of output data. But they were relatively insignificant compared to the major regions accounted for. The margin of error of this second possible source should not be serious.

The data on crude oil, though continuous, are not without defect. For the period 1912–24, there is only a single source of unknown quality (Chao P'ing, 1935, pp. 24–25). It is possible that the low output levels reported in this source result from the omission of the output of other production centers, but this conjecture has not been verified.

Electric power generation data are complete and reliable for most years. For the years between 1926 and 1936 data are unquestionably complete, but from 1937 to 1945 regional subtotals were aggregated. For lack of information, the Japanese-occupied regions, exclusive of Manchuria and North China, had to be left out. While the magnitude of error is not easily ascertainable, the estimated series again suffers from statistical omission. Finally, output for the years prior to 1926 was estimated by a roundabout method; details are given in Appendix A.

In summary, the series on mining and metallurgy are, on the whole, more complete and reliable than the others. In almost every case, data for the years prior to 1937, particularly 1927 to 1936, are better than for the later years. During the war years, data for the then Free China are the best among all regional data. Manchurian data during the war are scattered and incomplete, and there is almost no economic information

3. According to one source, Ch'i-hsin's output accounted for 100% of the cement produced by Chinese firms as late as 1919 (Nankai University Economic Research Bureau, 1963, p. 158). But there were smaller Chinese-owned cement companies in operation at that time—for example, Hu-peh, Shang-hai, and others—although their outputs were extremely low as compared to that of Ch'i-hsin (Hou Hou-p'ei, 1929, pp. 134–36).

about the other Japanese-occupied regions. On balance, the series are based only on carefully selected data, and the indexes are believed to be an adequate basis for an overall picture of China's industrialization, emphasizing its general trend and pattern of industrial development rather than the growth of individual industries.

The results of this research, as exhibited by the composite indexes of industrial production, conform in most cases to *a priori* expectations based on our general knowledge. From the descriptive literature, we know that modern industries underwent a period of rapid expansion in China during and immediately after World War I. A major setback was suffered in 1921 or thereabouts, when foreign enterprises and suppliers returned to the Chinese market as they recovered from the war. The Sino-Japanese War in 1937 severely disrupted industrial production in most areas. All of these ups and downs in the levels of industrial output are clearly borne out by the production indexes constructed on the basis of these 15 series. The reasonableness of the results, if taken as a whole, would suggest that the indexes derived and the conclusions based on them may provide a fairly adequate basis for analysis.

One important exception should be noted concerning the effect of the world depression on the Chinese economy during the 1930's. China was on the silver standard until the currency reform of November, 1935, and most of her trading partners were on the gold standard. The fall of the gold price of silver in the world market resulted in a depreciation of the Chinese currency. This protected the Chinese economy from the impact of the world depression after 1929. However, when the world silver price rose after 1932, and especially in 1934 when the United States government offered to buy silver at a price far above the world market price, the export of silver from China became profitable and inevitable. This silver drain produced severe deflationary pressures on the Chinese economy. (See

Cheng Yu-k'wei, 1956, pp. 216–17.) These changes in world economic conditions do not seem to have had much effect on the modern industrial sector of China. The indexes of industrial production during the 1930's, either inclusive or exclusive of Manchuria, show no decline. (See Table 27.) Production estimates for the modern manufacturing sector made by Liu Ta-chung (1946, p. 12, Table 3) also show an uninterrupted upward trend during the 1931–36 period. Yeh Kung-chia's index of industrial production (1964, p. 66, Table 4), including factories, mining, and utilities for 1931–36, also supports this conclusion.

ESTIMATION OF UNKNOWNS

In Appendix A a detailed account of the various estimating methods used is given. Here, we shall discuss briefly and in general terms the procedures followed and the results obtained.

Some of the estimates are simply the result of interpolation or extrapolation. This method was used only to a limited extent and as a last resort in cases where the gaps in the series were minor and after searching for all other possible means of estimation. In no case was it used uncritically—that is, taking an arithmetic mean of two figures without reference to other considerations.

Depending on the character of the series, the other estimating methods used differed from case to case. Without going into details, two cases are presented here to illustrate this problem: cotton yarn and cotton cloth production.

Several years' output in the series on cotton yarn were estimated. For 1926, one source (*Shen-pao nien-chien*, 1934, p. 686) shows that the amount of cotton consumed in spinning mills was 6,581,000 piculs.[4] Another estimate shows that about

4. One picul = 133⅓ lbs.

10 per cent of the cotton was wasted in the spinning process (Ou Pao-san *et al.*, 1947a, Vol. II, p. 90). On the basis of these estimates, the amount of yarn spun in 1926 was estimated to be about 5,922,900 piculs, which is equivalent to 1,974,000 bales of 400 pounds. This seems reasonable, when compared with the output figures reported for 1925 and 1927 (1,792,000 and 2,127,000 bales, respectively).

It was much more difficult to estimate the gaps in the cotton cloth series. One could scarcely find even crude estimates of cotton cloth production prior to 1925.[5] The problem was to choose an estimating technique that was theoretically sound and would produce reasonable estimates.

Output estimates were made on the basis of cotton yarn consumed in the mills. Data on cotton yarn consumption are available for the period 1912–20 (*Chung-kuo-nien-chien*, 1924, pp. 1445–46); data for 1921–26 are independent estimates made in this study. In order to estimate the amount of domestic consumption of cotton yarn, imports were added and exports subtracted from the amounts of cotton yarn produced domestically.

From this estimated series on domestic cotton yarn consumption, it was necessary to determine the amounts consumed in the weaving factories in order to estimate the amount of cotton cloth produced on the basis of certain estimated input-output relationships. According to one estimate (Ou pao-san *et al.*, 1947, Vol. II, p. 99; Yen Chung-p'ing, 1955, p. 310), about one-eighth of the domestically consumed cotton yarn was for nonweaving purposes. After this one-eighth was subtracted from total yarn consumption, the rest represented amounts consumed for weaving purposes. The next problem was to determine the amounts consumed in weaving factories and the amounts consumed by hand looms,

5. There are only three rough estimates made for 1915, 1917, and 1925. (See Table 1).

in order to take this differential into account in gauging cotton cloth production.

A number of such estimates of percentage distribution of yarn consumption have been made by different experts and for a number of years. For 1913, Ralph M. Odell (1916, p. 185) estimated that 2.7 per cent of the total yarn consumption was consumed by the mechanized looms. Fang Hsien-t'ing (H. D. Fong) estimated that about 21.5 per cent of the yarn was consumed in the weaving factories in 1930 (1934, p. 275). According to an estimate made by Yen Chung-p'ing (1955, p. 311), 27 per cent of the cloth produced was by power-driven looms in 1934–35. However, Ou Pao-san (1947a, Vol. II, p. 99) estimated that only about 8 per cent of the cotton yarn (exclusive of the amount consumed for nonweaving purposes) was consumed in the weaving factories in 1933. The estimates made for the 1930's are radically different; the discrepancies are mainly due to different estimating techniques and assumptions they used.

On the basis of these estimates, several attempts were made to determine the approximate percentage distribution of cotton yarn consumption in the modern and the traditional sectors. The Odell estimate for 1913 seemed reasonable and was taken as a reference point for projections. The next problem was to select a point for the 1930's in order to estimate the intervening points by means of an estimated trend of development in the cotton cloth industry. For 1915, 1917, and 1925, estimates of the output of cotton cloth in the factories had been made by three independent sources. (See Table 1.) These were used as checks and as a basis for selecting one of the three estimated percentage figures for the 1930's cited above. After comparing the three, we found that the trend line based on Ou Pao-san's estimate for 1933 yielded results that checked best with the three independent estimates. Odell's 1913 and Ou's 1933 estimates were thus selected as the end points for projecting a step-like trend of development between 1912 and 1926.

TABLE 1
ESTIMATES OF COTTON CLOTH
PRODUCTION, 1912–26

(1,000 bolts of 40 yards)

Year	Our estimates	Estimates made by others
1912	732	
1913	836	
1914	1,087	
1915	1,500	1,125
1916	1,765	
1917	1,628	1,500
1918	1,437	
1919	1,840	
1920	1,892	
1921	2,504	
1922	2,190	
1923	3,199	
1924	2,554	
1925	3,113	3,001
1926	3,764	

Sources for the estimates made by others:
  Data for 1915: Great Britain, Economic Mission, 1931 (pp. 54–55).
  Data for 1917: U.S. War Trade Board, 1919 (p. 77).
  Data for 1925: Yen Chung-p'ing *et al.*, 1955 (p. 130). (Original source: Chinese Cotton Millowners' Association.)

In other words, it was assumed that the amount of yarn consumed by power looms in 1913 was about 3 per cent of the total. By 1933, 8 per cent of the total yarn was consumed in the factories, according to Ou Pao-san's estimate. Thus, an estimated trend line would indicate that the amount of yarn consumption in the factories increased one percentage point approximately every three years. This comes very close to the estimates made by independent sources for the years 1915, 1917, and 1925. (See Table 1.)

In this section, only a few of the problems about the selection of estimating methods and the use of raw data in the estimating process have been discussed; Table A–2 of Appendix A contains a complete account of the methods used in estimating each series and their results.

WEIGHTS

In combining the individual output series, a weighting system must be chosen that reflects the relative importance of the various series included in the index. For general purposes, the weights will be in value term, but for special purposes, the weights could be expressed in many nonvalue terms. For example, man-hours worked per unit of product could be used to weight the quantity relatives, if the aim were to compare labor productivity. Similarly, power-consumption per unit of product is a useful gauge. In a country where the price structure is known to be distorted, the wage bill might be a good substitute.[6]

In this study, the weights are in value terms and the p coefficient in the chosen formula

$$\frac{\sum p_0 q_1}{\sum p_0 q_0}$$

will be both the unit price and the unit value-added of the product. With the unit price as the weight, the index will measure changes in the levels of gross output, representing an amalgamation of contributions made by the different industries aggregated. If the pattern of industrial production

6. For a discussion of this see Donald R. Hodgman, 1954; United States Board of Governors, Federal Reserve System, 1960 (pp. 36–38) and Chao Kang, 1965 (ch. 4).

remained stable over time, the use of this weight would prob-ably produce as good a result as any other weight. However, this is not the case for the period of China under investigation. It is preferable, therefore, to use net value-added as the weight, so that the possibility of distorting effects on the index, resulting from the changing pattern of production and the structure of relative prices, could be at least partially corrected.

Since the period under investigation is long, it is best to use three or more weight-base years rather than a single one. Originally, it was planned to weight the physical quantities with 1925, 1933, and 1952 net (or gross) value-added figures, thereby permitting an intertemporal comparison of industrial growth with different price structures. The attempt was quickly dismissed, when search of data showed that only 1933 value-added information was readily available.[7] For lack of related cost information it does not seem feasible even to attempt estimates for other years. Therefore, there is only one index based on value-added weights.

In chapter 4, a set of two indexes is presented. These two indexes are based on 1933 gross price and 1933 net value-added per unit, respectively. The former is a gross-value index and the latter a close approximation of the net-value index of industrial production. The other set of three indexes weighted by 1925, 1933, and 1952 gross prices is presented in Appendix C. Most of the value-added data used in this study are derived from Ou's estimates by dividing his net value output by units of output. Such derivations based primarily on Ou's estimates (1947a, Vol. I, p. 53) were carried out for the other commodi-ties in the indexes. Other price data used in this study are tabulated in Appendix B with detailed source references.[8]

7. There are 1952 value-added data in Liu Ta-chung and Yeh Kung-chia (1965), but they simply projected the 1933 net to gross output ratios into 1952. (See Table H–1 on p. 569 and the note on p. 571.)

8. Ou Pao-san (1947a) contains price data for a long list of commodities, but only for the year 1933. Recently, there have been at least two long-term

The use of value-added weights, and particularly a constant value-added weight, creates a number of technical problems and disadvantages. Over time, changes occur in quantity and quality, as well as in the types of inputs used in producing the final products, because of variations in the patterns of consumption and production. A reduction in the amount of ore used as raw material in a particular mining industry is an example. The production index based on a constant value-added weight of an earlier year is downward-biased, because such a reduction in ore input, given constant quantity of output, is not reflected in higher value-added by the industry concerned. On the other hand, there are industries in which the inputs used have improved in quality. If the quantities of such inputs and the resulting output remained constant, the index of production for these industries would tend to have an upward bias.

Even with constant quantity and quality of inputs used, a change in the efficiency with which materials and fuel are used could generate upward or downward biases in the indexes of production. In many industries the efficiency of material or fuel utilization has tended to rise over time. This tendency could produce downward biases in the indexes of production based on a constant value-added weight of an earlier year.

A related problem is that, in general, a change in the value of net output cannot be uniquely separated into a price change and a volume change. In other words, one can conceptually, but not statistically, split the pq product, so that the p component can be held constant and the changes in q observed over time. This problem arises not only with respect to a value

---

price compilations published in Communist China (one for Shanghai and the other for Tientsin, both dating back to the early years of the Republican period), but they cover only a few commodities. See Chung-kuo k'o-hsüeh yüan, Shang-hai ching-chi yen-chiu-so (Shanghai Economic Research Bureau, The Chinese Academy of Sciences), 1958; and Nankai ta-hsüeh, Tientsin ching-chi yen-chiu-so (Nankai University, Economic Research Bureau of Tientsin), 1958.

of net output, which is an aggregate over many individual products, but also in the simplest case possible, where a single raw material is transformed into a single final product. In this case, one could construct an index of net output by subtracting input at constant input price from output at constant output price. But the fact that the prices of input and output are held constant does not mean that the margin between them is also unchanged. Any change in this margin, resulting, for example, from changes in the technical input-output relations, could generate biases in the index constructed as a measurement of net output. The problem is much more complicated in the more usual case, where several inputs are converted into several final products. In view of this problem of indeterminacy in measuring the changes in the volume of net output at constant prices, it should be recognized that any index number represents, at best, only an approximation of the real measure.

CHAPTER THREE

The Coverage

COVERAGE OF OUTPUT SERIES

THE GAPS IN the series are mostly in the consumer goods industries. The food and beverage, cigarettes, matches, and flour-milling industries are not represented. Parts of the textile industry (wool and silk, etc.) also had to be left out because of lack of data. Paper, leather, and the like are completely uncovered, and the chemical industry is also excluded. Therefore, the production series included in the indexes fall far short of a fully representative and comprehensive measure of total industrial production. On the other hand, the value output of these 15 key commodities does represent a fairly large proportion of total industrial production.

Some notion of the extent to which China's total factory production has been accounted for by the 15 series in the 1930's is shown in Table 2. These estimates are undoubtedly crude and are produced here only to show the extent of coverage. On

TABLE 2

SHARE OF THE 15 SERIES IN INDUSTRIAL PRODUCTION

(millions of 1933 yuan)

	NET VALUE-ADDED IN FACTORY PRODUCTION				
	A	B	C	C/A	C/B
			(our		
Year	(Ou)	(Liu-Yeh)	15 series)	(per cent)	(per cent)
1931	566	—	320	57	—
1932	572	—	334	58	—
1933	651	928	370	57	40
1934	654	—	395	60	—
1935	663	—	442	67	—
1936	713	—	499	70	—

Notes:
   The estimates made by Ou underwent a number of revisions; the figures used here were his latest. Ou's figures originally included handicraft output; they have been adjusted to correspond to ours by assuming that (a) factory output was 27 per cent of total production during the period (see Ou Pao-san, 1947a, Vol. I, p. 12); and (b) mining by modern methods constituted about 80 per cent of the total, based on coal, iron ore, and pig-iron outputs in the 1930's (see Yen Chung-p'ing *et al.*, 1955, pp. 102–103). Liu-Yeh's mining figure was adjusted by using the same assumption, and their manufacturing output data needed no adjustment for our purposes here.

Sources:
   Ou Pao-san, 1949, p. 204.
   Liu Ta-chung and Yeh Kung-chia, 1965, pp. 141, 569, and 578.

the basis of the estimates made by Ou Pao-san, the 15 series do represent a high percentage of total factory production for the years 1931–36, with only minor year-to-year variations. This evidence makes it not unreasonable to postulate that these 15 commodities played a dominant role in China's industrialization during the prewar period. However, if Liu and Yeh's estimate for 1933 is taken as the basis for our calculations, the percentage accounted for by the 15 series diminishes, thereby reducing somewhat the significance of the conclusions drawn in this study.

The discrepancy between these two independent estimates of China's factory production for 1933 can be attributed to a number of factors. The Liu-Yeh study is not only more recent but also more thorough and detailed. Closer examination and comparison of the two estimates of net value-added in factory production has shown the following differences: (1) The Manchurian data in Ou's study are incomplete. (2) Output of some foreign firms was unreported in Ou. (3) The value output of Chinese-owned factories reported in Liu-Yeh was almost consistently greater than the corresponding figure found in Ou, although both used the same basic source material (D. K. Lieu's industrial census of 1933). The discrepancy between the two estimates can be explained partly by differences in statistical coverage and partly by differences in the price weights used.

At first sight, a 40 per cent coverage of output for 1933, as shown by Liu-Yeh's estimate, might appear too limited a basis for a national index of industrial production.[1] However, a 40 per cent coverage or even less is not uncommon in other studies of national industrial growth. In Arthur Burns' *Production Trends in the United States Since 1870* (1934, pp. 17–20), for example, the same type of data problem was encountered. Some areas of industrial production are completely unrepresented. There are many important gaps in the manufacturing sector. The paper industry, printing and publishing, lumber products, leather, petroleum refining, machinery, and other industries are not included. For 1925, one of the most recent years in the study, the coverage of the

---

1. Perhaps it should be pointed out here that the degree of coverage of the indexes could have been increased somewhat by including in them some of the questionable production series, because some of the series could be made complete and continuous only by relying extensively on interpolation and extrapolation to fill the gaps or to extend the series. The price that would have to be paid for increased coverage would thus have been decreased firmness of statistical foundation for the study.

manufacturing sector is only 22 per cent, and all of the series combined account for only about 40 per cent of total national industrial production. If the series based on some very in-direct measurements were omitted, Burns' coverage would be reduced to a mere 26 per cent of national industrial output.

Donald Hodgman, in his *Soviet Industrial Production, 1928-1951* (1954, pp. 81–82), had to face similar data prob-lems. Beginning in 1938, the supply of annual industrial production statistics was sharply curtailed by the Soviet authorities, and this policy continued into the post-World War II years. As a result, the coverage of Hodgman's index was reduced from 137 series in the base year 1934 to 22 series in the years 1940 and 1946–50. It was further reduced to 18 series in 1951. The value-added of his 22 selected production series accounted for about 45 to 49 per cent of total value-added in the Soviet industries between the years 1929–30 and 1937. The percentage of coverage in this index is reasonably high; but the representativeness of his 22 series may be questionable.

Finally, another monumental work on the growth of industrial production should be mentioned. Solomon Fabri-cant's *The Output of Manufacturing Industries, 1899–37* (1940, pp. 351–52) is no exception to the usual problem of incomplete statistical coverage of industrial products. When-ever the physical output data do not encompass all the products of the industry, Fabricant has regarded a product coverage of 40 per cent as sufficient to compute an index of physical output.

Apparently, although a product coverage of 40 per cent may seem too low, other authors have also regarded as accept-able for constructing an index of industrial production. It should also be emphasized that the 15 series included in our indexes represent reasonably well China's industrial structure, as will be shown in greater detail later.

Unfortunately, for the years before 1931 and after 1936, no satisfactory way has been found to estimate the coverage of our 15 series. Nevertheless, as far as data will permit, we will try to give some indication of the changes in coverage before and after the 1931–36 period.

These changes depend primarily on the changing composition of industrial production during the period concerned. They depend also on the relationship between the product series included in the indexes and those excluded for lack of data. Both the extent and the direction of the changes in coverage of the 15 series could perhaps be assessed by an analysis of production trends in the excluded sectors of industrial production. Such a task would require a detailed perusal of the descriptive or qualitative literature for even a glimpse of the state of the uncovered industries before and after the 1930's. Even then it would be practically impossible to account for all the omitted industries for a short period of time, let alone the entire 37-year period. Therefore, only a brief survey of some of the more important industries omitted from the indexes can be attempted here. It will be confined to factory output only, despite the fact that the handicraft output portion of some of these industries was extremely high.

Uncovered Industries

Cigarette Industry

The establishment of the British and American Tobacco Company and that of the Pei-yang Tobacco Company in 1902 marked the beginning of cigarette manufacturing in China.[2]

2. For a brief survey of the development of the cigarette industry in China see the following works: Shih-yeh-pu (Ministry of Industries), 1934 (pp. K 572 ff.); Kung Chün, 1933 (pp. 221–24); Chung-kuo k'o-hsüeh yüan (Chinese Academy of Sciences), 1958; Wu Ch'eng-lo, 1929 (Vol. 2, pp. 72–76); Yang Ta-chin, 1938 (Vol. 1, pp. 787–811); and H. M. Wolf, 1934 (pp. 90–104).

The industry did not achieve significant scale of development until World War I, when the Chinese market was relatively insulated from foreign competition. Nanyang Brothers Tobacco Company, a leading Chinese-owned cigarette manufacturer, was organized in 1906 in Hongkong, but the market for its products was limited to the province of Kwangtung and Southeast Asia until 1915–16. By 1916, its market was substantially expanded into the North, and branch offices and factories were established in a number of cities, including Shanghai, Hankow and Peking. (See Kung Chün, 1933, p. 222; Yang Ta-chin, 1938, p. 789.) The output of the company's Hongkong factory was increased markedly from 4,759 cases in 1912 to 18,609 cases in 1915 and 33,825 cases in 1917 (Chung-kuo k'o-hsüeh yüan, 1958, p. 19). This was certainly an impressive rate of growth, and it is reasonable to suppose that other smaller companies experienced similar gains during the same period. The industry continued its vigorous expansion during the 1920's and the early 1930's with a possible setback in 1922—an experience shared by almost every consumer goods industry in China (Chou Hsiu-lüan, 1958, p. 52). The trend of development of the cigarette industry is indicated by Tables 3 and 4.

The May 30th Incident in 1925 precipitated a boycott of goods imported from Great Britain, resulting in a mushrooming of small-scale Chinese cigarette manufacturing firms. From 1924 to 1925, cigarette imports fell substantially, and they have never regained their 1924 level. (See Table 3.) The decreased supply of foreign cigarettes must have been made up by corresponding increases in domestic production. Moreover, Table 3 seems to suggest that the industry experienced a continued expansion in the late 1920's, if most of the imported leaf was for cigarette-manufacturing purposes. It should also be pointed out that before 1925 the value of imported tobacco leaf was consistently less than that of manufactured cigarettes.

This trend was then completely reversed, and the gap between the two has widened ever since.

TABLE 3
CHINESE IMPORT OF
CIGARETTES AND TOBACCO LEAF,
1920–30

(1,000 taels)

Year	Cigarettes[a]	Tobacco leaf[b]
1920	22,030	12,939
1921	24,913	14,270
1922	28,339	13,220
1923	28,273	12,777
1924	27,650	24,640
1925	17,768	19,602
1926	20,765	25,575
1927	12,765	22,095
1928	25,126	34,384
1929	20,746	44,590
1930	21,725	43,511

Notes:
a. The value of cigarette import was maintained approximately at the level of 20 million taels per year during the period 1931–36.
b. The value of tobacco leaf import was maintained approximately at the level of 42 million taels per year during the period 1931–36.
Source:
Yang Ta-chin, 1938 (Vol. I, p. 801).

Partial output statistics in Table 4 definitely indicate that the cigarette industry in the Japanese-occupied region outside of Manchuria almost disintegrated during the Sino-Japanese War. During the war years, the Nanyang Brothers' Shanghai plant produced only a negligible fraction of its prewar output. The same company's Chungking plant produced about 2,000 to 3,000 cases per year during the war, a small amount indeed (Chung-kuo k'o-hsüeh yüan, 1958, p. 521). Meanwhile, the cigarette industry in Manchuria made virtually no progress in terms of the level of output during the war (Chang Ch'en-ta, 1954, Vol. II, pp. 242–43).[3]

To sum up, on the basis of this fragmentary information, it seems reasonable to say that the cigarette industry of China began to grow rapidly during World War I, experienced its greatest expansion in the mid-1920's, and continued to grow until the peak was reached in the early 1930's. The war in 1937 disrupted and in some cases destroyed the industry in most areas of China.

TABLE 4
OUTPUT OF CIGARETTES,
NANYANG BROTHERS TOBACCO
COMPANY, SHANGHAI PLANT,
1932–45

(cases of 50,000)

Year	Output	Year	Output
1932	98,731	1939	28,574
1933	116,474	1940	20,474
1934	113,964	1941	15,539
1935	109,887	1942	3,706
1936	97,763	1943	5,934
1937	63,079	1944	7,223
1938	27,430	1945	4,246

Source:
Chung-kuo k'o-hsüeh yüan, 1958 (p. 171).

Flour-Milling Industry

Probably the next most important omission from our index is the flour-milling industry. China, as one of the most important wheat-producing countries in the world, developed milling

3. Output during the 1937–44 period fluctuated around 390,000 cases per year; it declined to 245,000 cases in 1944.

tools and equipment as early as the Chou dynasty, but employment of modern technology dates back only to 1896. Modern mills were first established in the wheat-producing areas in such large cities as Shanghai, Wusih, Tientsin, and Harbin. Several of these mills were organized on a very large scale and with sizable capital resources. The largest and best known among the Chinese-owned mills was the Mao-hsin and Fu-hsin, a chain of 14 or so modern flour mills, founded and controlled by Jung Tsung-ching and family, the first of which was established in 1898.[4]

On the basis of what we know from the descriptive literature[5] the flour industry advanced rapidly during World War I, when American and European supplies were sharply curtailed and Russia and Japan depended heavily on China for flour. Trade statistics show that a substantial import surplus of flour in 1914 was converted into a slight export surplus in 1915. This export surplus continued to rise until a peak was reached in 1920. Then, the so-called Golden Age of flour milling came to an end with a shift back to a large import surplus in 1922. (See Table 5.) Throughout the 1920's, the industry stagnated.

A number of factors come readily to mind to explain the inherent weakness of the Chinese flour-milling industry. Foreign competition was, of course, a major factor and requires no elaboration. But the most important and decisive factor was the stringency of the domestic wheat supply. Up to 1922, China had maintained a wheat export surplus, but because of repeated crop failures, the tide was turned. The result has been a substantial wheat import surplus since 1923,[6]

4. See Mow Sing and Foh Sing Flour Mills and Sung Sing Cotton Mills, 1929.
5. See, for example, Yang Ta-chin, 1938 (pp. Vol. I, 621–45); Shih-yeh-pu, 1934 (pp. K 10 ff.); "Flour Mills in China," 1928 (pp. 533–42); and "Flour Industry in Kiangsu," 1933 (pp. 32–48).
6. "Flour Mills in China," 1930 (pp. 323–24).

the same year in which flour imports began to exceed flour exports.

The quality of domestic wheat was another serious problem. The domestic supply was often impure and wet, with a low powder content. (See Fang Hsien-t'ing, and Ku Yuan-t'ien, 1934, p. 74.) This led the Chinese-owned flour mills to depend more and more heavily on imported wheat. High internal transport costs and heavy taxation further intensified the domestic wheat supply problem.

On the basis of all of these indications combined, it seems safe to conclude that the flour industry expanded rapidly from 1915 to 1921 and began to decline after 1922. Beginning in 1932, the industry showed signs of revival, presumably because of the imposition of import duties on flour. Information about the industry's development during and after World War II is too limited to permit any appraisal of production trends.

TABLE 5

CHINESE IMPORT AND EXPORT OF FLOUR, 1912–31

(1,000 tan)

Year	Import (−) or export (+) surplus	Year	Import (−) or export (+) surplus
1912	− 2,565	1922	− 3,008
1913	− 2,458	1923	− 5,695
1914	− 2,110	1924	− 6,465
1915	+ 58	1925	− 2,495
1916	+ 56	1926	− 4,150
1917	+ 110	1927	− 3,707
1918	+ 2,007	1928	− 5,899
1919	+ 2,423	1929	− 11,909
1920	+ 3,449	1930	− 5,183
1921	+ 1,294	1931	− 4,864

Source:
Shih-yeh-pu, 1934 (pp. K 40–41).

Match Industry

Another important consumer goods industry omitted is the manufacture of matches.[7] This industry, too, had an early beginning in China. The first establishment was the Chu-ch'ang Match Company in Chungking in 1889. Others were founded later in Hankow, Changsha, and Shanghai (Yang Ta-chin, 1938, Vol. I, p. 513; Fang hsien-t'ing and Ku Yuan-t'ien, 1934, p. 97). Despite the number of fairly large Chinese-owned match companies from the early days, the market was almost completely dominated by the supply from various foreign powers. Prior to 1896, the market was dominated by European products; between 1896 and 1918, especially during World War I, Japanese matches prevailed. After 1927, the Chinese market was practically taken over by Swedish products. During 1918 and 1927 evidence seems to show that the domestic supply was sufficient (Shih-yeh-pu, 1934, p. K 561).

Under these waves of foreign competition, the overall position of the Chinese-owned companies remained relatively weak and insignificant during the period under consideration. However, due partly to repeated boycotts of foreign goods, the number of Chinese establishments increased steadily, especially in the early 1920's. By 1929, there were 185 Chinese-owned match companies scattered throughout the country (Fang and Ku, 1934, p. 97). Statistics on match output in China are extremely scarce. There are no long-term output series. Import statistics are, however, readily available, as shown in Table 6. They throw some light on development trends of the match industry.

Over the time period covered, match imports declined

7. For an account of the match industry see the following: Shih-yeh-pu, 1934 (pp. K 561 ff.); Yang Ta-chin, 1938 (Vol. I, pp. 507–39); Kung Chün, 1933 (pp. 197–207); Hou Hou-p'ei, 1929 (pp. 140–44); and Chao Ts'ung, 1935.

TABLE 6
CHINESE IMPORT OF MATCHES, 1912–33

(1,000 gross)

Year	Import	Year	Import
1912	30,090	1923	2,229
1913	28,448	1924	2,739
1914	28,836	1925	2,855
1915	20,973	1926	3,703
1916	20,621	1927	6,026
1917	15,594	1928	6,427
1918	13,341	1929	8,413
1919	16,599	1930	8,505
1920	8,484	1931	2,525
1921	4,307	1932	368
1922	2,703	1933	73

Source:
Inspection and Commerce, 1935 (p. 13).

almost consistently year after year. In addition to the boycotts, China's tariff autonomy was restored in 1931, and a 40 per cent import tariff was placed on matches. This, in combination with other factors, apparently brought about substantial gains in the supply of domestically produced matches. Growth of the industry is evidenced by rising imports of the raw materials used in match manufacturing, especially during the 1930's (Yang Ta-chin, 1938, Vol. I, pp. 526–27). This suggests that domestic output of matches experienced a continuous rise during the period 1912–36. Part of this increase was undoubtedly due to the expansion of foreign-owned enterprises in China.

In summary, the match industry of China seems to have had a firm foundation as early as the turn of the century, and it experienced a period of rapid expansion during World War I and into the early 1920's. The industry continued to grow in the 1930's until it was interrupted by the Sino-Japanese War in 1937. During the war, the industry declined both in Manchuria and in the interior. These developments are brought out in Table 7.

TABLE 7
PRODUCTION INDEXES OF MATCHES,
MANCHURIA AND FREE CHINA,
1938–44

Year	Manchuria	Free China
1938	100	100
1939	119	101
1940	88	124
1941	86	127
1942	76	489
1943	88	70
1944	55	73

Sources:
  The Manchurian index is based on Chang Ch'en-ta, 1954 (p. 243).
  For Free China: Bureau of Information, 1947 (p. 369).

Paper Industry

Much of China's paper-making activities were still in the traditional sector and were employing premodern methods during the period under investigation. In 1932, for example, combined factory production of paper and cardboards totaled approximately 37,000 tons, of which only about 8,000 tons was paper. (See Hsü Wu, 1934; "Chung-kuo chih-yeh tiao-ch'a pao-kao," March and April, 1940.) In contrast, handicraft paper production in the same year was estimated to be about 360,000 tons (State Statistical Bureau, 1958, p. 197).

Despite the fact that China had invented paper making as early as in the second century, the application of modern technology to the paper industry dates back only to 1891. This is marked by the establishment of the Lun-chang Paper

Company (later renamed T'ien-chang) by Li Hung-chang in Shanghai. Other modern paper manufacturing enterprises were established soon after that in Shanghai and other cities. As in many other industries, inefficient management and operation and poor capital resources and technical know-how impeded the development of the Chinese-owned firms. As a result, here again, the domestic market was dominated by foreign supplies.

The evidence indicates that the industry enjoyed a brief period of expansion during World War I, when a large number of modern factories were organized. But this period of relative prosperity was soon ended, when the foreign supply and enterprises returned after the war. (See, for example, Yang Ta-chin, 1938, Vol. I, p. 300.) Studies also show that the industry was in its infancy before 1930 and that it developed rapidly afterwards. Strictly speaking, however, modern paper manufacturing in China was insignificant throughout the prewar period, including the period of relatively greater development during the 1930's. The output of machine-made paper and cardboards was still very low during the 1930's. But the rates of growth in the 1930's were quite high, almost tripling in the five years from 1931 to 1936. (See Table 8.) This

TABLE 8

FACTORY PRODUCTION OF PAPER AND CARDBOARD, 1931–36

(1,000 tons)

Year	Output
1931	31
1932	37
1933	44
1936	89

Sources:
For 1931–33, see Hsu Wü, 1934.
For 1936, see State Statistical Bureau, 1958 (p. 198).

rapid rate of growth should have some effect on the index and the overall rate of industrial production.

In view of this background of low output and the inherent weakness in the modern manufacturing sector of China's paper industry, it is not difficult to conceive of a rising trend of paper imports during the prewar period. This is indeed shown in Table 9.

TABLE 9
CHINESE IMPORT OF PAPER, 1912–36

(1,000 tons)

Period	Annual average
1912–18	34
1919–1928	86
1929–32	187
1933–36	306

Source:
State Statistical Bureau, 1958 (p. 198).

On the basis of this evidence, it would seem reasonable to conclude that the increase in domestic consumption of machine-made paper during the prewar years was sustained mainly by increased imports, especially newsprint, for which China depended entirely upon foreign supplies (Yang Ta-chin, 1938, Vol. I, p. 302). Chinese import of paper increased rapidly after 1929, when, in the midst of economic depression, the foreign powers found China a good market for their surpluses. The paper industry of China could not compete with the cheaper and better-quality foreign products. This competition, and the lack of technological know-how, virtually precluded the possibility of domestic development of the industry during the prewar period.

The paper industry did make some progress in the interior

during the Sino-Japanese War, although much of the productive capacity in the Shanghai and Tientsin areas was destroyed. (See Chang Yung-hui and Chang Hsi-nien, 1942.) Table 10 shows this rapid rate of increase in paper production in the

TABLE 10

PRODUCTION INDEX OF PAPER IN FREE CHINA, 1938–44

Year	Index
1938	100
1939	107
1940	134
1941	257
1942	691
1943	583
1944	692

Source:
Bureau of Information, 1947 (p. 369).

TABLE 11

PRODUCTION OF PAPER IN MANCHURIA, 1937–44

(1,000 tons)

Year	Output
1937	22
1938	29
1939	37
1940	42
1941	58
1942	81
1943	84
1944	50

Source:
Northeast China Economic Commission, 1947 (Table 5).

interior. The level of output, however, remained extremely low. In 1943, for example, the output of machine-made paper in the then Free China was only about 10,000 tons (State Statistical Bureau, 1958, p. 200). In Manchuria, on the other hand, because of vigorous Japanese efforts, the paper industry made more important gains during the war. Table 11 provides a partial picture of this development.

Chemical Industry

Unlike the industries discussed earlier, the chemical industry of China (excluding matches), came into existence only in the late 1920's. Yang Ta-chin, in his 2,000-page study of China's modern industries, devoted less than three pages to a discussion of the chemical industry. Kung Chün (1933), another important source, allocated only two paragraphs to it, and Fang and Ku (1934), in their lecture outline on China's modern industries cited earlier, did not even include the chemical industry. According to Yang (1938, Vol. I, p. 113), the commercial production of various chemical compounds began in the late 1920's, and there were only four notable producers in China. Throughout Yang's work, one finds no mention of the production of gasoline, alcohol, and similar chemical products. The same is true of Kung Chün's and other studies on the history of modern industries in China. On the basis of this evidence, it would seem that the production of these chemical products was negligible during the prewar period.

After the outbreak of the Sino-Japanese War, the output of some of these products advanced quite significantly, at least in the interior. Responding to wartime military demands, the production of gasoline and alcohol was accelerated. Table 12 summarizes the situation in Free China. Impressive gains were also made in the production of other chemical products, including soda ash, caustic soda, bleaching powder, and sulphuric and hydrochloric acids (Bureau of Information, 1947, p. 369).

The record of performance of the chemical industry was not as impressive in other parts of China. In Manchuria, available data do not show any consistent pattern of change, either upward or downward, during the war years (South Manchuria Railway, 1942, pp. 20–21). This was true of North China too, except for the production of alcohol, which made rapid advances between 1938 and 1944.[8]

TABLE 12
PRODUCTION INDEXES OF
GASOLINE AND ALCOHOL IN
FREE CHINA, 1938–44

Year	Gasoline	Alcohol
1938	100	100
1939	104	264
1940	1,669	1,490
1941	4,029	1,767
1942	37,679	2,566
1943	65,497	2,427
1944	83,154	2,464

Source:
Bureau of Information, 1947 (p. 369).

Machinery Industry

This industry also had a very early beginning in China. The first foreign-owned ship-building factory was established in 1851, and the first Chinese-owned hardware factory in 1883 in Shanghai. After 1883, the number of machine-shop establishments increased rapidly, but most of these so-called

8. Wang Foh-shen, 1948b (pp. 8–9). The production index of alcohol rose from 100 in 1938 to 1,900 in 1944.

"machine factories" were no more than repair shops or hardware workshops which could produce only machine parts. The first Chinese-made machinery products appeared on the market in 1902 (Shih-yeh-pu, 1934, pp. C 599 ff; Chou Hsiu-lüan, 1958, p. 57).

Development of this industry depended heavily upon that of the other industries, chiefly textiles, flour and rice-milling, and silk-reeling. When the supply of foreign machinery was virtually cut off during World War I, and most of the consumer goods industries experienced rapid expansion, the demand for domestically made machines was greatly increased. The machinery industry, therefore, enjoyed a period of prosperity when other industries were expanding their scale of operation. It is for this reason that the machinery industry has been fittingly described as a "subsidiary to the other industries in a local area."[9]

However, under normal circumstances when the domestic machinery industry did not enjoy a protected status, as was the case during World War I, it faced insurmountable difficulties in attempting to develop and expand. Chinese industrialists, as a rule, lacked confidence in the locally made machines and preferred to invest in the more expensive foreign-made ones when they were available. The classic example of this was the China Iron Works Factory (Chung-kuo t'ieh-kung ch'ang), a firm established for the sole purpose of promoting the production and sale of Chinese-made machines and supported by the leading industrialists of Shanghai (Yang Ta-chin, 1938, Vol. I, p. 853). With these industrial capitalists as shareholders and potential buyers, it was hoped that the company would make a major contribution in supplying the machinery needed for industrialization. Unfortunately, these potential buyers failed to provide the

9. Chou Hsiu-lüan, 1958, p. 57 (translation mine).

encouragement required and showed no confidence in the company's products. All other firms faced the same handicap in varying degrees.

During the Sino-Japanese War years, the machinery industry flourished in Free China, and production of generators and motors increased very rapidly (Bureau of Information, 1947, p. 360). However, virtually nothing is known about the development of this industry in other parts of China during this period.

CONCLUSIONS

The foregoing account, however incomplete, of the industrial sectors omitted from the index should indicate some of the effects of these exclusions on the movement of the index over time. Among the omitted sectors surveyed, the cigarette, flour-milling, and match industries—or, to generalize, the consumer goods industries—show a trend of development similar to that of the composite index. The only exception is the flour industry during the 1920's. The chemical, machinery, and paper industries did not begin production until the late 1920's and developed only in the 1930's and during the war years.

For a more precise analysis of the problem, the structure of China's factory production has been estimated in Table 13. From the table we may observe that some of the omitted series, such as machinery, chemical, paper, and many other small industries not listed, represented only tiny fractions of China's total industrial production in 1933. However, some of these industries, especially the machinery and chemical industries, made substantial gains in their relative positions by the late 1930's and in the 1940's. The textile industry, as well as the omitted food-processing and cigarette industries, declined substantially in their relative importance during the war,

1937–45, according to the descriptive literature. During World
War I and even in the early 1920's, the machinery and chemical
industries probably accounted for even smaller fractions of
total industrial production.

It would seem, therefore, that the coverage of our series is
probably greater than 40 per cent of the nation's total industrial production for the years prior to the 1930's. This seems
especially true during and immediately after World War I,
when some of the omitted industries had not even been

TABLE 13
STRUCTURE OF MODERN INDUSTRIES, 1933

Industrial groups and products	Total net value-added (per cent)	Total gross value-added (per cent)
Textile products	20.9	22.0
(cotton yarn and cloth)	(17.2)	(17.2)
Food	5.2	6.8
(flour)	(2.4)	(1.7)
Cigarettes	4.0	11.2
Metal products	4.1	3.7
(iron and steel)	(2.3)	(1.8)
Machinery	0.7	1.2
Paper	1.1	0.6
Chemical	3.8	3.6
(matches)	(1.7)	(1.8)
Mining	30.0	19.9
(coal)	(13.4)	(9.5)
Utilities	21.7	14.4
(electric power)	(17.4)	(10.9)
Others	8.5	16.6
Totals	100.0	100.0

Sources:
    Net value-added: Ou Pao-san, 1947 (Vol. I, p. 54 and Table 2).
    Gross value-added: based on Liu Ta-chung and Yeh Kung-chia, 1965
(Tables F–1, F–4, H–1, and H–4).

started. After 1937, the output of the consumer goods industries declined sharply, while the omitted industries made
increasing gains in importance, both in absolute and in relative
terms. The 40 per cent coverage for 1933 must be much
reduced for the war years, and the 15 series may be less
representative of the nation's industrial production for those
years when the omitted series were rapidly expanding.

It is clear that the index varies in strength over the time
period concerned. In general, it is relatively strong before
1937, especially between World War I and 1936, but its
strength is substantially reduced after 1937. These findings
would naturally affect the rates of industrial growth as
calculated in chapter 5 for the entire period, as well as
for several selected subperiods. For the post-1936 period,
when some of the omitted industries made great advances, the
growth rates would tend to be biased downward. In other
words, by leaving out some of these rapidly expanding industries the index has understated the actual rate of growth of the
industrial sector after 1936. On the other hand, the direction of
bias resulting from incomplete coverage for the pre-1936
period is not certain, but at least two possible sources of bias
can be identified.

First, the newly developed industries omitted in the index
may have experienced very high rates of growth, although this
cannot be documented satisfactorily. The inclusion of these
industries would undoubtedly increase the rates of growth
calculated for the periods concerned. However, since their
weight was still small in 1933, the effect would not be very
significant. Second, although the flour-milling industry,
together with other consumer goods industries, experienced
fast growth during World War I, it stagnated throughout the
1920's. Had it been possible to include this industry in the
index, the growth rates for the 1920's might have been lower
than those shown by the index. In net value-added terms,

however, the flour industry had only a very small weight in total industrial production. (See Table 13.) Whatever the bias might be, it could not be serious. Since, like the flour industry, most of the sectors included in our index expanded rapidly during World War I, our index is not subject to the second type of bias for the period before 1920. During the 1920's, both of these biases are present, but their net effect on the composite index is not certain, since they operate in opposite directions. It should be emphasized, however, that neither of these two biases is significant.

In summary, it is quite clear that the index does not overstate the actual rate of industrial production up to 1920; for the 1920's and the subsequent years through 1936, there would seem to be no significant biases in either direction; and after 1936, at least during the war years, the index definitely understates the actual rate of industrial growth.

CHAPTER FOUR

Indexes of Industrial Production

THE CONSTRUCTION OF the indexes reflects the availability of both output and price data. It should be reiterated here that the unit price and value-added data for all 15 commodities are available for only one year—1933. For 1925 and 1952, selected as comparison base years, unit price data are available for only 14 commodities. Therefore, two sets of industrial production indexes have been constructed, both ranging from 1912 to 1949. This chapter presents the two indexes based on 15 commodity series weighted by 1933 net value-added and gross prices, respectively. An attempt is made to compare the results of this study with those of Wang Foh-shen and Fred C. Hung. The indexes based on 14 commodity series weighted by 1925, 1933, and 1952 gross prices are found in Appendix C.

OUR INDEXES

The index weighted by unit gross prices is, in a sense, a gross output index, and the one weighted by unit net value-added is a net output index ("net" in the sense indicated in the first chapter). Table 14 presents these two indexes on which Chart 1 is based.

Chart 1 clearly shows that the two indexes almost coincide with each other up to 1936. This indicates that there was little or no change in the pattern or composition of production during that period. After 1936, the two do show discrepancies. The gross index reached its peak in 1936, dropped substantially when the war broke out in 1937, and then recovered rapidly, but not to the 1936 level. The net index also peaked in 1936, but, after a temporary decline, continued its upward trend until it attained its highest level in 1942. This was considerably higher than the 1936 prewar peak.

Discrepancies between the two indexes can be measured more exactly by comparing the net value output with the gross value output over the range concerned. For this purpose, the ratio of net value output to gross value output for all years has been calculated, and the ratios for some years are presented here for illustration. From Table 15 we observe that during the period under study the ratio fluctuated around 0.3 and 0.4, except for the wartime years. This indicates that the relationship between gross and net value of output before the war was reasonably stable. When the war broke out, this norm was disturbed, and the ratio fluctuated from 0.43 in 1937 to 0.56 in 1942 and remained at that level until 1945.

The ratio for each commodity does not change, since constant 1933 weights have been used. The discrepancies in the aggregate ratios (Table 15) can therefore be explained, at least in part, by examining the changing structure of industrial production during the period under investigation. In this respect, special attention was given to those commodities which are relatively more material-using. For this purpose the ratio of net value-added to gross value per unit of output for each of the 15 commodities was computed. This ratio ranges from a low of 0.22 for cotton cloth to a high of 1.00 for mercury. Since those commodities which are relatively material-using would tend to have a low ratio, the two lowest have been selected for further examination. As expected, these are cotton cloth and cotton yarn, with ratios of 0.22 and 0.24, respectively.

These two commodities, ranking among the most important of all industrial products, constituted a high percentage of China's total industrial production. Based on the net value-added of the 15 commodities in 1933, the changing importance of these two commodities in the total is reflected by the ratios shown in Table 16.

TABLE 14

INDUSTRIAL PRODUCTION OF MAINLAND CHINA, 1912–49

(15 commodities)

Year	Gross value of output		Net value-added	
	(millions of 1933 yuan)	(Index 1933=100)	(millions of 1933 yuan)	(Index 1933=100)
1912	119.6	11.9	58.0	15.7
1913	157.4	15.6	71.1	19.2
1914	201.9	20.1	88.9	24.0
1915	226.3	22.5	96.7	26.1
1916	241.5	24.0	102.5	27.7
1917	270.9	26.9	118.2	32.0
1918	279.5	27.8	119.2	32.2
1919	343.1	34.1	136.3	36.9
1920	404.6	40.2	158.5	42.9
1921	427.1	42.4	156.7	42.4
1922	348.9	34.7	144.1	39.0
1923	418.9	41.6	168.7	45.6
1924	471.7	46.9	186.7	50.5
1925	560.4	55.7	222.3	60.1
1926	594.2	59.0	225.6	61.0
1927	670.1	66.6	245.1	66.3
1928	725.6	72.1	260.8	70.5
1929	773.8	76.9	278.2	75.2

TABLE 14 *continued*

Year	Gross value of output (millions of 1933 yuan)	(Index 1933=100)	Net value-added (millions of 1933 yuan)	(Index 1933=100)
1930	821.1	81.6	296.4	80.1
1931	886.9	88.1	320.0	86.5
1932	921.5	91.6	334.1	90.3
1933	1,006.3	100.0	369.7	100.0
1934	1,042.6	103.6	395.0	106.8
1935	1,104.1	109.7	441.8	119.5
1936	1,227.4	122.0	499.1	135.0
1937	966.1	96.0	415.5	112.3
1938	766.8	76.2	385.0	104.1
1939	887.7	88.2	446.5	120.7
1940	947.0	94.1	508.8	137.6
1941	1,098.8	109.2	596.3	161.2
1942	1,164.5	115.7	651.2	176.1
1943	1,062.8	105.6	581.1	157.1
1944	923.4	91.8	521.3	140.9
1945	624.3	62.0	348.1	94.1
1946	912.6	90.7	346.3	93.6
1947	1,158.4	115.1	432.1	116.8
1948	972.7	96.7	374.1	101.1
1949	1,062.9	105.6	440.7	119.2

Sources:
Appendixes A and B.

It is interesting to note the high degree of negative correlation of the ratios in Table 16 with those in Table 15. Put another way, movements in the gross value measure of industrial production depend heavily on changes in the output levels of the more material-using commodities. The higher the rates of growth of the material-using commodities, relative to the total, the higher will be the level of total gross output, and the greater the discrepancies between the gross and net indexes.

As the war broke out in 1937, the textile industries of

CHART I Indexes of
Industrial Production of Mainland China, 1912-1949
Gross and Net Output (15 Commodities)
(1933=100)

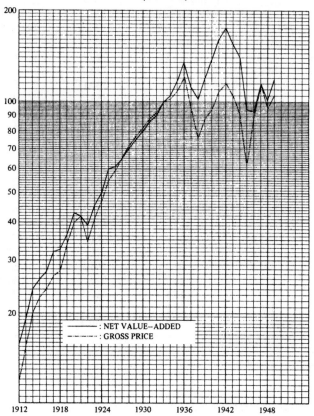

China (exclusive of handicrafts) almost completely disintegrated, and output dropped dramatically. As a result, the gross output index, as shown in Chart 1, went far below the net output index, which is not affected nearly as much by the behavior of the material-using industries. Throughout the war years, the textile industry failed to regain its prewar output levels. On the contrary, as a percentage of total industrial production, the combined output of these commodities

TABLE 15

TOTAL NET VALUE-ADDED AS A PER CENT OF TOTAL GROSS VALUE
OUTPUT, 1912–49, SELECTED YEARS

Year	Per cent	Year	Per cent	Year	Per cent
1912	0.48	1933	0.37	1942	0.56
1917	0.44	1936	0.41	1944	0.56
1921	0.37	1937	0.43	1945	0.56
1925	0.40	1938	0.50	1946	0.38
1929	0.36	1940	0.54	1949	0.41

Source:
Table 14.

TABLE 16

VALUE OF COTTON YARN AND CLOTH OUTPUT AS
A PER CENT OF TOTAL INDUSTRIAL PRODUCTION
(1933 net value-added)

Year	Per cent	Year	Per cent
1921	44.1	1940	8.7
1933	41.6	1942	5.4
1936	30.7	1945	5.3
1938	12.5	1946	37.5

Sources:
Table 14 and the appendixes.

declined almost steadily during the period, as shown in Table 16. In terms of a comparison of the gross and net indexes shown in Chart 1, the gap between the two widens during these years. By 1946, when the textile industry finally regained its prewar importance, the two indexes again converge.

In conclusion, we may say a word on the reliability of these indexes. For the prewar years, 1912–36, the two indexes are equally good for interpretative purposes, given their common shortcomings and limitations. After 1936, when the raw data become not only more scarce but also less reliable, the net output index is to be preferred for analytical applications.

Comparison with Other Indexes

The 1933 net value-added index constructed in this study, though crude in nature, is by far the most complete and comprehensive one available for pre-Communist Mainland China. As mentioned in chapter 1, there have been a number of industrial production indexes constructed for China, differing in time span and product coverage. A comparison of some of these might be interesting and useful.

Fred C. Hung (1958), for example, has constructed an index of industrial production for six major commodities—cotton yarn, cotton cloth, pig iron, steel, coal, and cement—from 1922 to 1936. This, as far as is known, is the only attempt made in the United States to provide a long-term industrial production index for China. The Hung index is tabulated and compared in Table 18.

Liu Ta-chung (1946, pp. 44–52) also estimated China's industrial production, but only for 1931–36. The trend of industrial growth shown by Liu's index agrees reasonably well with ours for the same period. Another short-term index of industrial production for 1931–36, including factories, mining, and utilities, was estimated by Yeh Kung-chia (1964, Table 4, p. 66), and it shows a similar upward trend.

In China, several different indexes were constructed. The Central Bank of China (1939, p. 1632) constructed an index of industrial production for the 1930's for a number of key consumer goods, including cotton yarn, cigarettes, flour, matches, cement, and beer. This effort was discontinued when the war broke out. During the war, the Department of Statistics of the Ministry of Economic Affairs (Central Bank of China, 1946) compiled and published industrial production indexes for a much wider range of commodities, but this was confined to the then "Free China."

Wang Foh-shen (1948a), a principal collaborator of Ou

Pao-san, constructed an index which has been considered to be the best and most comprehensive. The Wang index covers eleven principal commodities from 1931 to 1946. (See Table 17.) Close scrutiny indicates at least two significant shortcomings. First, although the index was supposed to be national in scope, the raw output data covered Free and North China only. The two regions on which the index was based accounted for only 23 per cent of the nation's total industrial output in 1933 (Wang, 1948a, p. 11). Moreover, Free China, under the government's continued effort to industrialize, experienced rapid industrial expansion during the war years, while the Japanese-occupied regions, exclusive of Manchuria and North China, remained in a crippled condition. Therefore it is grossly misleading to assume, as Wang does, that the industrial development of the country as a whole could be represented during the 1931–46 period by developments in Free and North China alone.

Secondly, the methodology employed by Wang in constructing the composite index is erroneous. In order to clarify this point, Wang's individual and general indexes for four selected war years, 1942–45, are reproduced in Table 17. It should be noted that his general index registers a continuous rise over this four-year period, while some of the individual indexes depart greatly from the general index. In calculating his general index, Wang simply took an arithmetic average of the indexes of the eleven series, without applying any weighting factors to the series aggregated. While the resulting general index might conceivably reflect the trend of development in the wartime interior, the methodology used is theoretically unsound.

In addition to these two significant shortcomings, there are many other minor defects. Among the 11 commodities chosen, which account for about 40 per cent of the country's industrial output in 1933 (Wang, p. 4), 5 are chemical products,

TABLE 17
WANG'S PRODUCTION INDEXES,
1942–45
(1942 = 100)

	1943	1944	1945
Pig iron	105	139	143
Steel	75	45	55
Cement	86	79	80
Electric power	132	147	155
Alkalis	88	59	53
Sulphuric acid	69	121	78
Hydrochloric acid	114	125	109
Alcohol	98	101	204
Gasoline	170	214	227
Cotton yarn	100	94	79
Flour	94	79	74
General index	103	109	114

Source:
Wang Foh-shen, 1948a (p. 10).

suggesting that the representativeness of the Wang index is open to question. Furthermore, the alcohol and gasoline series showed extremely high growth rates during the war years. Given Wang's methods of index construction, the degree of bias introduced by the production trends of these two commodities alone must have been quite significant. Finally, Wang's index for the years 1931–32 and 1934–36 is based on employment rather than output data.[1]

Table 18 tabulates the indexes constructed by Hung and Wang along with the author's net output index for 15 commodities. The three indexes are plotted in Chart 2. The Hung index is constructed along the same lines as the author's

1. In addition to this major undertaking, Wang has also constructed separate wartime industrial production indexes for North China and Free China. See his article in *Ching-chi p'ing-lun* (1948b, pp. 7–11).

TABLE 18

A COMPARISON OF THE INDUSTRIAL
PRODUCTION INDEXES BY HUNG, WANG,
AND CHANG

(1933 = 100)

Year	Hung	Wang	Chang
1922	46.8	—	39.0
1923	53.4	—	45.6
1924	57.3	—	50.5
1925	57.9	—	60.1
1926	61.8	—	61.0
1927	68.3	—	66.3
1928	76.3	—	70.5
1929	79.1	—	75.2
1930	82.4	—	80.1
1931	89.9	87.3	86.5
1932	91.0	90.5	90.3
1933	100.0	100.0	100.0
1934	110.1	104.8	106.8
1935	119.6	117.4	119.5
1936	136.6	125.4	135.0
1937	—	106.4	112.3
1938	—	57.1	104.1
1939	—	77.8	120.7
1940	—	106.4	137.6
1941	—	119.0	161.2
1942	—	158.7	176.1
1943	—	163.7	157.1
1944	—	173.0	140.9
1945	—	180.9	94.1
1946	80.4	119.0	93.6

Note:
— stands for not available.
Sources:
Fred C. Hung, 1958.
Wang Foh-shen, 1948a (p. 10).
Table 14.

CHART 2 Three Indexes Compared: Hung, Wang, and Chang
(1933=100)

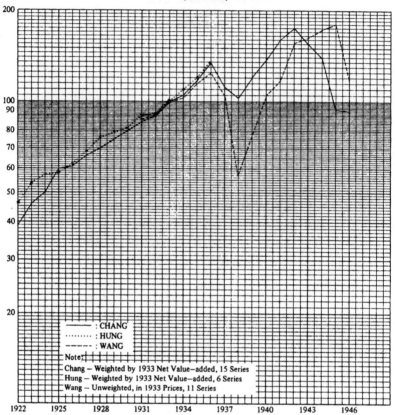

——— : CHANG
········· : HUNG
———— : WANG

Note:
Chang — Weighted by 1933 Net Value—added, 15 Series
Hung — Weighted by 1933 Net Value—added, 6 Series
Wang — Unweighted, in 1933 Prices, 11 Series

differing only in coverage. For the years compared, Hung's index agrees with the author's in a general way, with only minor year-to-year discrepancies. Wang's index differs from the author's not only in product and geographical coverage, but also in methodology. Chart 2 shows that the author's index reaches its peak in 1942 and then starts to decline. The Wang index rises from the trough of 1938 and continues to rise until 1945. The trend of development shown by Wang's index is not representative of the country as a whole, though for the war years it depicts fairly well the efforts made by the National Government to industrialize the territories under its control, mainly the southwestern interior.

CHAPTER FIVE

Rate and Pattern of Industrial Development

IN THE PRESENT chapter the rates of growth and the pattern of development are analyzed on the basis of the 1933 net value-added index. As mentioned previously, it should be borne in mind that this index does not include handicraft production but does encompass Manchuria's industrial output.

RATES OF GROWTH

The average annual growth rates for the entire period under discussion, 1912–49, as well as for selected subperiods, are shown in Table 19. The rates for the entire period are not as meaningful as those for the various subperiods, since neither 1912 nor 1949 were in any sense normal or representative years. The data for 1912 are relatively unreliable compared to those for the later years. In 1949 the country was in a highly chaotic state, and as a result much of the industrial capacity was idle.

The subdivision of the 1912–49 period requires a word of explanation. It was hoped that the divergent growth rates of the different subperiods would illustrate the growth tendencies of each period according to its characteristics and circumstances. The index indicates that 1920 was the year when

TABLE 19

AVERAGE ANNUAL RATES OF INDUSTRIAL
GROWTH, 1912–49 AND SUBPERIODS

(per cent)

Periods	Growth rate
1912–49	5.6
1912–20	13.4
1912–36	9.4
1912–42	8.4
1923–36	8.7
1923–42	7.4
1926–36	8.3
1928–36	8.4
1928–42	6.7
1931–36	9.3
1931–42	6.7
1936–42	4.5

Source:
Table 14.

China's World War I boom reached a peak, following a period of substantial industrial expansion during and immediately after the war. 1923 was taken as a normal year after the post-World War I recession which, according to the index, began in 1921. For the pre-Sino-Japanese War period, industrial production in China, including Manchuria, reached its peak in 1936. 1942 marked the wartime peak, or the peak over the entire pre-Communist period. The reason for choosing 1928 as a benchmark year is that the National Government was established in Nanking in that year, and relative political stability was attained and maintained from then until the outbreak of the Sino-Japanese War in 1937. Socioeconomic reforms and modernization programs were also launched in this period. Beginning in 1931, a number of important public policy measures designed to promote the growth of domestic industries were put into effect.

Over the entire period, 1912–49, the average annual rate of industrial growth is 5.6 per cent, a rate lower than that for most of the subperiods. In 1949 the level of economic activity was approximately equal to that of 1935 and substantially below the wartime peak of 1942. (See Table 14.) The period begins with a relatively low base (1912 = 15.7), and also ends in a year when the nation had not yet regained its prewar output level and capacity—thus producing the low rate of average annual growth for the entire period.

The growth rate over the 1912–20 period is the highest among those calculated. During this period, especially during World War I, foreign competitors diverted their attention, though only temporarily, from Chinese markets. War broke out in 1914, and the European powers converted their production facilities from civilian to military needs. Meanwhile, foreign shipping was also converted to military use. Chinese imports from these countries dropped substantially and in some cases were cut off completely. Even after the war, the European powers could not recover sufficiently to return to the Chinese market immediately. As a result, the domestic industries of China made substantial gains during this period. The rate for this period is 13.4 per cent, while that for the 1912– 36 period is lower—9.4 per cent. Admittedly these rates are biased upward through the use of the relatively low comparison base of 1912.[1]

In order to minimize this potential upward bias, the comparison base years are shifted forward. The year 1928, for example, was not only one in which the political situation became much more stable, but also one in which the groundwork for the compilation of more comprehensive industrial statistics was being laid. Moreover, by 1928 the output levels for a number of key industrial commodities were nearing their prewar peaks. There can be little or no upward bias of the type mentioned when 1928 is used as the reference base. The rate for the period 1928–36 is 8.4 per cent, still a very impressive record of industrial expansion.

A still later and better year can be chosen, but at the expense of reducing the length of the time period concerned. The year 1931 can justifiably be regarded as one of the ideal and most representative prewar years that can be used as a reference base. The growth rate calculated for the relatively short 1931–36 period is 9.3 per cent. Based on this evidence, it would seem safe to conclude that before the Sino-Japanese War a representative average annual rate of growth for the modern industrial sector of the Chinese economy was in the

1. To correct this problem partially, annual growth rates based on three-year averages have been calculated to compare with the single-year rates shown in Table 19:

Periods	Growth rate
1912/14–1947/49	5.1%
1912/14–1919/21	11.0
1912/14–1935/37	8.3
1912/14–1941/43	7.6
1922/24–1935/37	8.0
1922/24–1941/43	7.1
1925/27–1935/37	6.9
1927/29–1935/37	7.1
1927/29–1941/43	6.2
1930/32–1935/37	7.4
1930/32–1941/43	6.1
1935/37–1941/43	5.1

neighborhood of 8 to 9 per cent. Data for the wartime and postwar years are less than adequate enough to warrant further elaboration concerning the average annual rates of growth.

PATTERN OF DEVELOPMENT

The evidence suggests that the industrial growth of pre-Communist China could hardly be characterized as long-term stagnation or retardation. For the 1912–36 period China experienced almost uninterrupted industrial expansion at a reasonably high rate. Total industrial production increased approximately eight times,[2] but the rate of increase of the various industrial products included in the study was quite uneven, and the rate of expansion of any one of these industrial products differed from period to period. Therefore, the relative importance of individual products in the country's total industrial output changed over time. The purpose of this section is to examine the changing composition and structure of the industrial sector during the period concerned.

For this purpose most of the 15 individual products have

2. For the wartime years, 1937–45, only fragmentary observations are possible because of the lack of national statistical data. According to the author's index of industrial production, the growth rate for the period 1938–42 was 14.1 per cent, reflecting mainly the rapid advances achieved both in the interior and in Manchuria. In addition, the following regional indexes of industrial production for Free and North China during the war years are worthy of note:

Year	Free China	North China
1938	100.0	100.0
1939	162.6	135.5
1940	300.2	144.8
1941	337.8	138.6
1942	417.0	154.0
1943	608.8	155.5
1944	633.8	183.3

Note:
Converted from the original 1942=100.
Source:
Wang Foh-shen, 1948b (pp. 9–10).

been classified into subgroups, and the percentage contributions of each to the total industrial product over the 1912–49 period has been calculated. The results show that there was no clearly observable pattern of continuous or consistent transformation over the period as a whole. During some of the subperiods, however, gradual shifts in industrial structure may be observed. For this reason, it would be better to center our attention on some of these subperiods, or some of the benchmark years. These gradual changes may be brought out most clearly by dividing the 1912–49 period into three subperiods, with this division centering around the Sino-Japanese War.

Table 20 shows that consumer goods accounted for only 21.9 per cent of the total in 1912, but this percentage increased to 44.1 by 1921. This high percentage was maintained until the early 1930's. Therefore, the most important branches of industry were consumer goods during the first subperiod of 24 years.

Meanwhile, the relative contribution made by the electric power series to total production increased steadily during the first subperiod, rising from 3.3 per cent in 1912 to 22.1 per cent in 1936.

Although the production of ferrous metals recorded the greatest gains in terms of rate of advance, it remained relatively insignificant throughout the subperiod. The relative contribution made by coal production showed no significant change over the subperiod. Its percentage in the total fluctuated around an average of about 25 per cent.

The production of "other mining products" was the only area that clearly and unmistakably declined in terms of relative contribution to the total. In 1912, the output of this group accounted for 40.0 per cent of total production, but by 1936 it contributed only 8.6 per cent. However, this by no means represents an absolute decline in the output of these products.

TABLE 20
RELATIVE IMPORTANCE OF KEY INDUSTRIAL GROUPS
SELECTED YEARS

(per cent of total net value-added in 1933)

Period	Year	Consumer goods	Coal	Ferrous metals	Other mining products	Electric power
	1912	21.9	31.2	1.5	40.0	3.3
	1917	29.2	31.0	7.2	25.6	3.7
	1921	44.1	29.8	7.7	11.7	5.4
I	1922	32.7	34.1	6.8	16.3	7.3
	1926	40.6	24.2	4.5	15.6	12.0
	1930	44.3	23.5	5.3	8.9	13.5
	1933	41.6	20.9	5.2	7.4	20.2
	1936	30.7	23.7	8.5	8.6	22.1
	1937	25.4	26.4	13.0	11.4	16.1
II	1940	8.7	30.5	13.8	9.5	23.6
	1943	5.7	30.4	19.5	3.1	32.3
	1945	5.3	26.4	5.0	3.9	50.4
III	1946	37.5	16.5	0.7	4.7	37.7
	1949	29.3	24.6	3.3	3.3	35.2

Note:
  Consumer goods: cotton yarn and cotton cloth; ferrous metals: iron ore, pig iron, and steel; other mining products: antimony, copper, gold, mercury, tin, and tungsten. Cement and crude oil, accounting for only negligible fractions of the total, have been omitted; the percentages, therefore, do not add up to 100.

It only indicates that the rates of growth for this group were lower than those of the other products.

Next we consider the wartime period from 1937 to 1945. Again, the relationship between coal production and total output was a stable one over the years, while the relative importance of other mining products continued to decline to a mere 3.9 per cent in 1945. Relative electric power output forged ahead until a peak of 50.4 per cent was achieved in 1945. This comparatively strong position does not signify continued expansion of this industry; it only shows that during the war years output reduction in electric power was relatively less than in other products.

Most characteristic of this period was the decisive shift in the orientation of the wartime economy. The production of ferrous metals and electric power gained relative importance in the aggregate at the expense of consumer goods output. The percentage for consumer goods began to decline in the late 1930's. This trend continued throughout the war years, and in 1945 these products contributed only 5.3 per cent of the total.

The absolute production decline of consumer goods branches was equally dramatic; taking 1933 = 100, it fell to 12.1 in 1945 (Table 21). In addition to the rapid advances made in the production of ferrous metals and electric power, the output of other strategic and producer goods (such as chemicals and machinery, not included in the index) also made great strides during the war.[3]

The postwar subperiod was too short and too chaotic to be appraised; furthermore, some of the output data for the period are the result of interpolation and other crude estimation procedures. Instead of looking at this subperiod as a whole, it would be better to center our attention on specific events that took place during these years and their impact on the changing pattern of industrial production at the end of World War II.

Available evidence shows that from 1945 to 1946 the economy was "reoriented" toward the production of consumer goods. During the war years, when the nation's resources were organized mainly for military and strategic uses, the consumer goods industries, as represented by cotton textiles,

3. For details see Wang Foh-shen, 1948b; Ching-chi-pu (Ministry of Economic Affairs), 1941; and Bureau of Information, 1947 (pp. 361–86).

almost vanished in the Japanese-occupied areas.[4] Although great efforts were made to evacuate some of the existing plants and equipment from the coastal areas to the interior, the move was not well prepared and organized and encountered a host

TABLE 21
INDEXES OF PRODUCTION, KEY INDUSTRIAL GROUPS, 1912–49

(1933 net value-added)
(1933 = 100)

Year	Consumer goods	Coal	Ferrous metals	Other mining products	Electric power
1912	8.3	23.5	4.7	84.7	2.5
1913	12.1	25.9	29.3	85.0	3.3
1914	16.2	36.3	37.2	90.2	3.7
1915	19.2	38.6	41.9	89.4	4.6
1916	20.7	43.2	46.1	85.4	5.2
1917	22.4	47.7	44.5	110.9	5.9
1918	24.0	50.6	49.3	98.5	6.8
1919	32.9	58.2	60.3	81.0	7.2
1920	39.5	64.3	70.2	98.9	7.8
1921	44.9	60.7	62.9	66.8	11.4

4. For example, flour output in Shanghai factories fell to 22.3 (1936= 100) in 1941, according to one source. (See Wang Foh-shen, 1948a, p. 5). Similarly, the declining output of cotton yarn in Shanghai factories during the war years is described by the following set of production indexes:

Year	Index
1936	100.0
1937	65.0
1938	42.4
1939	68.2
1940	73.9
1941	65.5
1942	9.1
1943	4.3

Almost identical patterns of development were true of the output of cotton cloth in Shanghai factories. Finally, it should be borne in mind that the Shanghai area was the major producing center for both cotton textiles and flour before the outbreak of the war. (See Economic Research Bureau of Shanghai, 1945, p. 194.)

TABLE 21 *continued*

Year	Consumer goods	Coal	Ferrous metals	Other mining products	Electric power
1922	30.6	64.0	51.3	85.8	14.1
1923	38.5	77.2	48.7	74.1	21.3
1924	44.5	84.2	51.9	66.4	27.7
1925	53.6	79.8	48.7	142.0	34.0
1926	59.6	71.1	53.4	128.5	36.2
1927	69.7	80.5	59.7	111.7	37.2
1928	76.3	81.8	69.7	98.9	42.5
1929	80.9	85.8	76.5	96.0	49.0
1930	85.3	90.5	81.7	96.4	53.6
1931	91.7	95.9	78.6	106.9	62.0
1932	93.7	91.9	89.1	85.0	86.3
1933	100.0	100.0	100.0	100.0	100.0
1934	98.1	117.4	114.8	103.7	111.6
1935	93.5	136.9	187.1	129.2	128.0
1936	99.5	153.8	223.7	157.7	148.3
1937	68.6	142.7	283.0	173.0	89.9
1938	31.4	130.8	289.2	196.7	112.3
1939	37.6	157.8	323.8	198.9	113.6
1940	28.9	201.8	368.4	117.0	160.7
1941	32.0	252.2	438.1	186.9	187.6
1942	22.7	265.6	540.2	160.6	224.4
1943	21.6	229.6	595.3	65.7	251.8
1944	16.5	232.2	402.4	44.5	256.3
1945	12.1	119.6	90.6	50.0	235.2
1946	84.4	74.4	12.0	59.1	174.9
1947	108.1	79.8	19.9	65.0	225.4
1948	86.4	56.5	16.8	69.7	216.5
1949	84.0	140.9	75.5	52.6	207.8

Sources: Appendixes A and B.

of technical difficulties. On the other hand, neither the interior nor Manchuria had ever been significant producing areas for these consumer goods.[5] Consequently, the production of

5. Manchuria's share of cotton yarn production, for example, was only about 4 per cent of the nation's total during the 1930's. (See Appendix A for details.)

consumer goods as shown by our production index declined more or less continuously during the war years. (See Table 21.)

With the end of war in 1945, the Chinese government acted almost immediately to take over Japanese-owned or -controlled factories and plants in the occupied areas, including Manchuria. Despite the difficulties of readjustment during the transitional period in the first half of 1946, output statistics clearly suggest that the rate of plant reopening or production resumption was reasonably high. As a result, the prewar level of output for the consumer goods industries was regained in 1947, as shown by the consumer goods production index (Table 21).[6] The output of "other mining products" was practically unaffected by these developments and remained insignificant during the postwar period. (See Tables 20 and 21.)

The output levels of the remaining three categories underwent substantial changes from 1945 to 1946, as shown in Table 21. Some of these changes were unprecedented. The output of coal, ferrous metals, and electric power all declined, not only in volume of production but also in their relative contribution to total industrial production. The production of ferrous metals declined most sharply, as shown by the index in Table 21.

The major producing center of these strategic industrial products during the war years was Japanese-occupied Manchuria. Undoubtedly, the productive capacity of these industries was damaged by bombing. Industrial production in these and other areas must have been seriously interrupted and possibly even broke down completely during the fourth quarter of 1945. However, for these strategic products, the rate

6. Information on this transitional and chaotic period of postwar years is seriously lacking. For a partial picture, see the section on "Industry" in *Chung-kuo ching-chi nien-chien, 1947*.

of output decline was much greater from 1945 to 1946 than from 1944 to 1945, as a glance at Table 21 will readily show. The output of the ferrous metals group, for example, dropped to 12.0 in 1946 from 402.4 in 1944 and 90.6 in 1945 (1933 = 100). This drastic rate of decline over so brief a span was, to a somewhat lesser extent, also characteristic of coal and electric power production during the postwar years. While the decline from 1945 to 1946 can be explained partly by war damage and transitional difficulties, the major factor was unquestionably Soviet removals of industrial plant and equipment from Manchuria.

According to the report made by Pauley (1946, p. 7), "the difference in condition of the Manchurian industrial plant between Japanese surrender and the dates the Pauley Mission made its survey is appalling. How much of the wrecked condition is a direct result of Soviet removals, and how much may be ascribed to pillage, civil war, and other indirect consequences of the Soviet occupation cannot be accurately determined. In any case, the Soviet government must bear the major responsibility." The Soviets entered Manchuria on August 9, 1945, and the Japanese surrendered on August 14. Soviet removals of industrial plant and equipment started in early September. They took mainly the operationally more efficient and newer equipment and left the older behind.

The Pauley Mission estimated that the total loss amounted to U.S. $895,000,000. Later in 1946, under the auspices of the Chinese government's Northeastern Industrial Association and the Japanese Rehabilitation Liaison Office, a team of 21 Japanese experts who held key positions in Manchuria made further investigation into the matter. The Japanese mission's estimate of losses in the areas accessible to the mission amounted to U.S. $1,236,211,000, in terms of prewar prices. Losses in the inaccessible areas due to fighting between Nationalist and Communist forces amounted to at least 50 per cent of this figure. Therefore, according to the Japanese mission, the total loss of industrial plant and equipment was about two billion U.S. dollars (Chinese Association for the United Nations, 1952, p. 1). The extent varied from industry to industry. Estimates of capacity reduction made by these two missions are presented in Table 22.

In light of these unusual events, we can not really characterize the postwar Chinese industrial development as "re-oriented" toward the production of consumer goods. All we can say, based on fragmentary evidence, is that the consumer goods industries were rehabilitated or reactivated faster and earlier than the heavy or the producer goods industries in the Japanese-occupied areas of China proper, while in Manchuria industrial capacity was crippled by Soviet occupation and removals. The wartime interior, which was oriented toward

TABLE 22

REDUCTION IN INDUSTRIAL CAPACITY BY SOVIET REMOVAL

(per cent)

Industries	Pauley estimates	Japanese estimates
Electric power	71	60
Coal mine	90	80
Iron and steel	50–100	60–100
Railway	50–100	50–100
Mechanical industry	80	68
Liquid fuel and lubricant	75	90
Chemical	50	33*
Nonferrous metal	75	50–100
Textiles	75	50
Pulp and paper	30	80
Telecommunications	20–100	30

Source:
Chinese Association for the United Nations, 1952 (pp. 3–4).
* Food etc.: 50%.

producer goods, was virtually deserted after the government returned to Nanking, since its wartime economy developed and flourished mainly on military and other government contracts.

In conclusion, it is evident that in Mainland China the modern industrial sector was mainly centered on consumer goods before 1936. While other industrial branches, such as ferrous metals and electric power, moved ahead year after year, they did not overtake the consumer goods industries in their relative importance. On the other hand, wartime industrial output, reflecting mainly the developments in the interior and in Manchuria, was unquestionably producer goods-oriented.

Finally it must be borne in mind that the foregoing analysis is based on the outputs of the 15 commodity series included in the index. What is known about the uncovered sector, however, suggests that China's prewar industrial development was even more consumer goods-centered and wartime industrial production more producer goods-oriented than would appear from the 15 series.

A different way of observing the changing or shifting pattern of industrial development in Mainland China is to compare the average rates of growth of the individual industrial products. For this purpose, average annual growth rates for the five industrial branches have been calculated over several time periods. The results are shown in Table 23. From the table, we observe that the growth rates for coal production correspond fairly closely to that of total production (cf. Table 19), while the growth record of "other mining products" was not at all impressive.

The trend of development of the consumer goods industries, as represented by cotton yarn and cloth, has been one of rapid expansion in the early years and retardation during the war. During 1912–36, for example, this group expanded at an

TABLE 23

AVERAGE ANNUAL RATES OF GROWTH, SELECTED INDUSTRIAL
GROUPS AND PERIODS

(per cent)

Periods	Consumer goods	Coal	Ferrous metals	Other mining products	Electric power
1912–49	6.5	5.0	7.8	−1.3	12.6
1912–20	21.6	13.4	40.2	2.0	15.3
1912–36	10.9	8.1	17.7	2.6	18.4
1912–42	3.4	8.4	17.1	2.1	16.0
1923–36	7.6	5.4	12.8	6.0	15.9
1923–42	−2.7	6.7	13.5	4.1	13.2
1928–36	3.4	8.2	16.3	6.0	16.6
1928–42	−8.3	8.8	15.7	3.5	12.6
1931–36	1.6	9.9	24.3	8.1	18.5
1931–42	−11.9	9.7	19.2	3.8	12.4
1936–42	−21.8	9.5	15.0	0.3	7.5

Source:
Table 21.

annual rate of 10.9 per cent, but during 1936–42, it contracted at a rate of 21.8 per cent per year.

It is interesting to note that the rates of growth in ferrous metals and in electric power were most rapid, with these two industries experiencing a parallel development, at least up to the wartime peak year. This parallelism is reflected by their expansion in absolute rates of growth, as well as by their gains in relative position in the total. (Compare Tables 20 and 21.)

It is also noteworthy that the growth rates in the consumer goods branches were somewhat lower before the war than those in ferrous metals[7] or electric power, except for the 1912–20 period, and that these rates became negative during the wartime period. On the other hand, the growth rates in ferrous metals and in electric power showed no marked change from period to period. In view of these comparative growth rates, it may be argued that the consumer goods branches advanced relatively faster than the others during the prewar period. This evidence, in part at least, supports the observation made earlier that China's prewar modern industries were more or less consumer goods-oriented.

Two Qualifications

The foregoing analysis of the rates and patterns of industrial development in pre-Communist China, as represented by the 15 selected commodity series, must be viewed not only in light of the trend of development of the uncovered industrial sectors discussed in chapter 3, but also in the light of two further qualifications.

Handicraft Sector

The first qualification concerns the problem of handicraft displacement in the process of industrialization.[8] That is, it is necessary to examine and determine whether the modern sector—and factory industries in particular—developed at the expense of the traditional sector—handicraft output in particular. Strictly speaking, there are two closely interrelated

7. It should be pointed out here that the growth rates of this group for the periods with 1912 as the base year are not necessarily meaningful, since the output level of ferrous metals in 1912 was abnormally low. (See Appendix A of this study for details.)

8. I am deeply indebted to Professor Alexander Eckstein for calling my attention to this problem and its relevance to this study.

questions or, perhaps, just two aspects of the same problem.

One aspect of the problem is whether the growth and development of the modern sector resulted in an absolute decline in the output of the traditional sector, particularly handicraft production. If so, then total net industrial growth will be necessarily slower than the growth of the modern sector alone. The other aspect of the problem is whether the growth of the modern sector leads only to a relative displacement of the handicraft sector. That is, in the process of industrialization, both factory industries and handicraft activities may be expanding. However, since the latter typically expands at a slower rate, it may decline in relative importance.

If we approach the problem by examining and comparing the growth tendencies of different branches or types of the handicraft sector, entirely different impressions and conclusions might emerge. In other words, while some branches of the handicraft industry may be declining, other branches may be expanding in the process of industrialization. More importantly, new types of handicraft activities may emerge as a response to a host of internal and external stimuli present in a country undergoing industrialization and economic modernization.[9]

It is beyond the scope of this study to consider further these general questions and their implications for economic development. The primary task at this point is to develop a rough quantitative assessment of the degree of handicraft displacement, if any, resulting from the rapid expansion of China's modern industrial sector. Possibly another way of stating the problem is that the task is to find out as fully as possible the extent to which the rapid rate of growth of China's

9. Here we may have stepped into the elusive area of defining the "handicraft industry." Perhaps these new types of "handicraft activities" should be characterized as small-scale factory industries or cottage-industries which, are quite different from the traditional handicraft industry strictly defined. For a study of this definitional problem, see Lu Ch'ung-tai, 1963.

modern industrial sector, at least for the prewar period, would have to be modified if handicraft production, which presumably expanded at a lower rate than the industrial sector as a whole, were to be included in total industrial production.

In the case of pre-Communist China, this is made difficult by the lack of quantitative information concerning the handicraft sector; and there has been very little serious investigation of this problem. The common belief, as expounded by political thinkers and leaders, has been that foreign economic penetration and domination of China disrupted agriculture and, in absolute terms, displaced the output of the handicraft industries. A recent study by Hou Chi-ming (1965, ch. 7 and pp. 218–19) has attempted to refute these arguments with quantitative evidence to the contrary. One of the major hypotheses presented by Hou is that the industrialization process in pre-1937 China did not lead to an absolute displacement of the traditional or indigenous sector of the economy, even though its share in total industrial output declined and, for some branches, the rate of growth was relatively low.

Data on Chinese handicraft production are fairly complete for 1933. Ou Pao-san and Liu Ta-chung and Yeh Kung-chia have made various estimates. Data for other years during the period under investigation are extremely scanty, and, therefore, only a rough assessment of the problem of handicraft displacement can be attempted here.

As late as the 1930's the Chinese economy was still dominated by the traditional sector. According to Ou Pao-san (1947, p. 93), agriculture accounted for 61.5 per cent of China's net national product in 1933. Liu and Yeh's estimate (1965, Table 8, p. 66) shows that the net value-added in agriculture was 65.0 per cent of net domestic product in 1933. Traditional elements also prevailed in banking, trade, and transportation. The primary preoccupation here, however, will be with the

share of handicraft production in total industrial output.
Table 24 summarizes the estimates made by Ou Pao-san
concerning the relative importance of the handicraft portions
of total production in various industries in 1933. The average
for all industries was 72 per cent in 1933. According to Liu
and Yeh, handicraft production accounted for 67.5 per cent
of the net value-added in industry (including factory production, mining, and utilities only so as to correspond to the
coverage of "industrial production" in this study) in 1933.
These two estimates differ in statistical coverage,[10] but they

TABLE 24
RELATIVE IMPORTANCE OF HANDICRAFT PRODUCTION
AS PER CENT OF NET VALUE-ADDED IN 1933

Industry	Per cent
Wood products	95.1
Machinery	32.6
Metal products	32.6
Electrical appliances	11.4
Transportation equipment	91.8
Stone and earthenware	78.5
Chemicals	37.4
Textiles	62.9
Apparel	83.2
Rubber and leather	73.6
Food, beverage, and tobacco	90.3
Paper and printing	70.6
Scientific instruments	52.8
Miscellaneous	92.6
All industries	72.0

Source:
Ou Pao-san, 1947 (Tables 3 and 4, pp. 139–42).

10. An important difference in coverage of these two studies should be
pointed out. Ou includes in the factory sector only those manufacturing firms
employing 30 or more persons and using mechanical power, while Liu and
Yeh include all firms using mechanical power, irrespective of the number of
employees.

unmistakably point to the fact that the structure of industrial production in China in the 1930's was predominantly handicraft.

Estimates of handicraft production as a share of total industrial output are not readily available for other years and, if available, they are not necessarily comparable to the Ou or Liu-Yeh estimates for 1933. The only such estimate found in the literature for the pre-Communist period, other than 1933, was made by a research team which, in 1954, conducted a national survey of individual handicrafts in Mainland China. According to this estimate (Chung-kuo k'o-hsüeh yuan, 1957, p. 252), the value of total industrial production in the factories was 10.8 billion Chinese dollars in 1949, of which 2.9 billion represented the output of factory-type handicraft workshops. In addition, the value of handicraft output in 1949 was estimated to be 3.2 billion Chinese dollars. The share of handicrafts, therefore, was 43.5 per cent ($6.1 billion/$14.0 billion) of total industrial production in 1949.

Unfortunately, there are no national income estimates or industrial production data for the country as a whole for the 1940's, when the level of industrial production reached the pre-Communist peak. The industrial production data for 1952 may perhaps be used as a substitute for China's pre-1949 peak output. According to the 1954 survey mentioned above, the share of handicrafts (including factory-type handicraft workshops, as well as other types of handicrafts, individual and collectivized) was 35.8 per cent of total industrial production in 1952. Liu and Yeh (1965, p. 66), on the other hand, estimated that the handicraft's share in 1952 was 51.3 per cent of total industrial production (including factories, mining, and utilities).

It is therefore very difficult to make intertemporal comparisons on the basis of these various estimates. First, national estimates of this kind are completely lacking before 1933;

this limits such comparisons to the post-1933 period. In addition, estimates of the share of handicrafts made for 1949 are necessarily biased upward by the fact that most of the modern sector declined during the postwar period and had not regained its prewar level by 1949. The share of agriculture in 1946 still accounted for more than 65 per cent of the nation's income, according to Ou Pao-san (1948, p. 204). The share of handicrafts would appear to have been correspondingly high.

Finally, the year 1952 may not be a good substitute for the pre-Communist peak reached in the 1940's, since, during the wartime years, the country was made up of three distinct regions: Manchuria, other Japanese-occupied areas, and the interior. The development characteristics and importance of handicrafts were vastly different in these regions. In highly industrialized Manchuria, the share of handicrafts would probably be low, compared to other sectors. Japanese-occupied China was vast in area, but its boundaries changed frequently, and, in quantitative terms, it is an unknown area. Much of the industrial base in Shanghai and Hankow, for example, was either destroyed by war or successfully removed to the interior. Whatever industrial activities remained during the war were probably of the handicraft type. If statistical information for the war years were available for the area, the share of handicrafts would probably show an upward bias because of the lack of other industrial activities.

The wartime interior, or more broadly the areas under the control, however loosely at times, of the National Government in Chungking, is particularly interesting from the point of view of handicrafts. Several organizations, both government and semi-government, were set up during the war to promote industrial and economic development. Among these, the Chinese Industrial Cooperatives, known as C.I.C or Indusco, was credited with having made great contributions to China's wartime industrialization. Its major function was to organize and mobilize refugee craftsmen, who would otherwise be unemployed or underemployed, into cooperative units both in the then "Free China" and in guerilla areas of the Japanese-occupied territories.

Judging from the descriptive literature, particularly the pictorial posters displayed at that time, the bulk of the production activities in these cooperative units were handicraft in nature. Members of the cooperatives were engaged in manufacturing towels on hand looms, wool blankets with the abundant wool supply in the Northwest, umbrellas, bamboo products, and so on, as well as other marketable products requiring simple mechanical equipment.[11]

By June 1942, near the peak of the cooperative movement, there were a total of 1,590 industrial cooperatives scattered all over the country, including some in the front areas. The total membership reached 22,680 (Chen Han-seng, 1947, p. 41). If these cooperative members can be assumed to represent the total labor force in industrial cooperative handicraft undertakings, they must be considered fairly unimportant when compared to the 241,662 workers reportedly working in the 3,758 factories registered with the Ministry of Economic Affairs in the interior alone (Ching-chi-pu, 1943, p. 11). In terms of capital investment, the industrial cooperatives appear even less significant.[12] Of course, the information is far too fragmentary to provide a basis for a definitive statement about the share of handicrafts in the industrial structure, even for the wartime interior. Nevertheless, what quantitative evidence there is seems to suggest that the share of

11. For a comprehensive summary account of the C.I.C., see Chen Han-seng, 1947.

12. In 1942, capital paid-up in the industrial cooperatives totalled about 4.5 million Chinese dollars, while the amount of capitalization in the factories was nearly two billion Chinese dollars. (See Ching-chi-pu and Chen Han-seng).

handicrafts in total industrial production declined during the post-1933 period.

In an attempt to illuminate this problem further, a few commodity series that distinguish between modern and traditional output are presented in Table 25. Sources for the data on coal, iron ore, and pig iron are cited at the bottom of the table. The figures for cloth output produced by modern methods are the same as those used in constructing our index,

TABLE 25

PRODUCTION BY MODERN AND TRADITIONAL METHODS,
SELECTED COMMODITIES AND YEARS

Year	Coal (million m.t.)		Iron ore (million m.t.)		Pig iron (million m.t.)		Cotton cloth (million bolts)	
	M	T	M	T	M	T	M	T
1912	5.2	3.9	0.2	0.5	*	0.2	0.7	22.8
1917	10.5	6.5	0.6	0.5	0.2	0.2	—	—
1922	14.1	7.1	0.9	0.5	0.2	0.2	—	—
1927	17.7	6.5	1.2	0.5	0.3	0.2	—	—
1933	22.1	6.3	1.9	0.4	0.5	0.1	28.3	63.1
1937	31.4	5.8	3.4	0.4	0.8	0.1	—	—
1949	31.0	1.4	0.6	*	0.2	*	30.2	4.2

Notes and Sources:
    Coal, iron ore, and pig iron: 1912–37—see Yen Chung-p'ing, *et al.*, 1955 (pp. 102–103); 1949—Chao Kang, 1965 (pp. 120–21).
    Cotton cloth: see the text.
    —not available
    * negligible

and the sources of data and the methods of estimation are given in detail in Appendix A. The estimates for cotton cloth produced by traditional methods, however, are rough and must be explained here.

Ralph M. Odell (1916, p. 185), who made studies of cotton textiles for nearly every cotton-producing country in the world, estimated that in 1913 China's yarn output was about 200 million pounds. Import of cotton yarn was about 358 million pounds, and there was no export. The amount of yarn available for domestic consumption was, therefore, 558 million pounds. He further estimated that not more than 15 million pounds were consumed by power looms. The amount of yarn consumed on the hand looms was, therefore, about 543 million pounds. But Odell did not make an adjustment for the yarn consumed for nonweaving purposes, which has been estimated to be about one-eighth of the total domestic yarn consumption (or about 70 million pounds in this case). (See Ou Pao-san, 1947, Vol. II, p. 99.) On the basis of these estimates, the amount of yarn consumed for weaving purposes in 1913 should be about 488 million pounds, of which 473 million pounds (96.9 per cent of the total) were consumed on the hand looms. Assuming that this percentage distribution in yarn consumption was usable in allocating total cloth production by modern and traditional methods, the output by modern methods as estimated in this study, 0.7 million bolts (see Appendix A, Table A–2), would represent 3.1 per cent of total cloth production, and the output by traditional methods could correspondingly be estimated at 22.8 million bolts (*i.e.*, 96.9 per cent of the total).

For the 1930's, there are two separate estimates. Yen Chung-p'ing (1955, p. 310) has a percentage distribution estimate of yarn consumption for weaving purposes by modern and traditional methods. According to Yen, 63 per cent of the yarn was consumed on the hand looms in 1934–35 (a two-year average). H. D. Fong made a similar estimate for 1930, but, like Odell, he did not make an adjustment for yarn consumed for nonweaving purposes. He estimated that about 75 per cent of the yarn was consumed on the hand looms in 1930. On the basis of these two estimates, it has been assumed that the percentage of yarn consumed on the hand looms in

1933 was somewhere between 63 per cent and 75 per cent, or about 69 per cent. This provides the basis for the estimate of cotton cloth produced by hand looms shown in the table.

For 1949, the percentage distribution of cotton cloth production reported by Chao Kang (1965, p. 124) was taken and applied to the amount of production by modern methods, arriving at the estimated 4.2 million bolts produced by hand looms in 1949. From the estimates shown in Table 25, it is clear that the modern sector was expanding at a considerably higher rate than the traditional sector, at least up to 1937.

The estimates clearly show that the shares of production in the traditional sector, as represented by these four commodities, declined from 1912 to 1949, but the two sectors coexisted reasonably well before the war. In other words, despite the fact that there was some steady relative displacement of the traditional sector by the rapid advances achieved in the modern sector, there was relatively little absolute displacement before 1937. The traditional sectors in iron ore and pig iron were small to begin with, as shown by the figures, so that the extent of any displacement could not be significant. The trend of development represented by the coal series prior to 1937 does not provide a firm basis for making any conclusive

TABLE 26
BENCHMARK INDEX OF INDUSTRIAL PRODUCTION,*
FACTORY AND HANDICRAFTS

(net value-added)

	FACTORY PRODUCTION		FACTORY AND HANDICRAFTS	
Year	*Millions of 1933 yuan*	*Index 1933 = 100*	*Millions of 1933 yuan*	*Index 1933 = 100*
1912	20.0	14.0	78.5	28.3
1933	143.4	100.0	277.4	100.0
1949	167.8	117.0	180.2	65.0

* Based on the four series mentioned in Table 25.

statements concerning the problem of displacement. The prewar estimates of cotton cloth production certainly show a dualistic pattern of development in that industry.

Based on the adjustments made for handicraft production in the four series listed above, a benchmark index of industrial production including handicrafts was constructed (Table 26). Adjustments are made for only four series[13] because data are lacking for any meaningful adjustments in the other mining series. Persumably, there are no traditional sectors in the steel and electric power industries, and to a large extent this is also true of the cement industry. The only omission of any significance is the cotton yarn series. According to one estimate (Yen Chung-p'ing, 1955, p. 309), the traditional sector of cotton yarn production was 17 per cent of the total in 1934–35.

We may now qualify, however roughly, the rates of industrial growth for the modern sector calculated in the early part of this chapter. The average annual growth rates for 1912–33 and 1912–49 are 9.8 per cent and 5.9 per cent, respectively, in the modern sector alone, on the basis of the four series. (The corresponding rates of growth on the basis of 15 series are 9.3 per cent and 5.6 per cent, respectively.) The growth rates for the same two periods are 6.2 per cent and 2.3 per cent, respectively, when the handicrafts are included in total industrial production.

13. Estimates of factory production in Table 26 are based on the figures contained in the appendixes. Total production estimates are made by adding handicraft output onto factory output, using 1933 net value-added as weights. The results are as follows:

Net Value-Added in Factory and Handicrafts
(millions of 1933 yuan)

Year	Coal	Iron ore	Pig iron	Cotton cloth
1912	31.7	2.1	4.7	40.0
1933	99.3	6.7	16.0	155.4
1949	113.5	1.7	6.6	58.4

One important defect in the adjusted benchmark index is that the same set of price weights has been applied to both factory and handicraft production. Marketable handicraft products are typically of inferior quality and therefore should command a lower price when compared to the same product made by modern methods. Lack of adequate price information makes separation between the two impossible. There are, of course, instances in which the finished product manufactured by one method cannot be distinguished from that produced by another method. While the indiscriminate application of price weights to the handicraft output series may have overestimated the value of handicraft production, it should not introduce any biases into the calculation of the adjusted growth rates, since the growth rates are affected only by changes in the volume of production when constant weights are used.

Apart from these quantitative indicators of the extent of handicraft displacement, there is widespread but fragmentary evidence showing that several other handicraft industries were being displaced during the period under investigation. Strictly speaking, however, the displacement could not be attributed wholly to the rapid growth of modern industry. There are at least two separate yet closely interrelated factors contributing to this process: changes in the pattern of international trade and changes in the composition of domestic consumption.[14]

A case of handicraft displacement by foreign competition coupled with changing consumer habits is clearly demonstrated in the case of Chinese brush pen manufacturing. (See

14. There are, of course, other characteristics of the process of industrialization, or "modern economic growth," to use a term coined by Simon Kuznets. In his *Six Lectures on Economic Growth* (1959, Lecture I), Kuznets listed four major characteristics associated with the process of modern economic growth. In a more recent work (1966, pp. 490–500), which summarizes his research to date on the long-term records of economic growth, there is a

P'eng Tse-yi, 1957, Vol. 3, pp. 57–59.) For centuries this was probably the only writing instrument in China. According to one source, the brush pens manufactured in the province of Hunan at one time monopolized the entire Chinese market. At the peak of the industry's prosperity, they were even exported to Japan and other countries. But when the imports of pencils, fountain pens, and later the "Atom" pens (meaning ball-point pens) flooded the Chinese market, even the average schoolboy, at least in the cities, would wear a "Parker 51" in his shirt pocket and carry his brush pen to school only for calligraphy classes.

Similar cases of displacement are represented by the hand-spun textiles, embroidery, tobacco, leather-processing, knitted goods, silk reeling, china and ceramics, and so on (Peng, Vol. 3, pp. 17–28, 42–43, 55–56, 60–62, 401–102, 414–15, 501–509). This list is selective rather than complete. Moreover, the exports of a group of 13 major handicraft products, including cloth, pottery, china, leather, paper, etc. declined steadily during the prewar period (Peng, Vol. 3, pp. 64–65). However, this evidence may be inconclusive because export declines could be due to increased domestic consumption.

In summary, both quantitative and qualitative evidence suggests that the share of handicrafts declined in total industrial production during the period under discussion. Nevertheless, the Chinese economy in the 1930's was still dominated by handicraft methods of production. The pressures associated with or generated by the economic modernization process

---

selective list of 15 common characteristics of modern economic growth. It is not the intention of this study to review or discuss the general subject of structural change associated with the process of economic development in this section, but these two characteristics have been singled out for closer examination because they appear to be the two relevant features of the Chinese case. For a general discussion of the subject on structural change, see Kuznets, 1966, especially ch. 3; for the Japanese case in particular, see W. W. Lockwood, 1954, ch. 8.

were very strong on certain branches of the handicraft sector, but other branches coexisted very well with the modern sector. This is in part due to the persistent demand for cheap and inferior handmade products by the masses, at least in the prewar period. The rapid expansion of the modern industrial sector was responsible only in part for the displacement of handicrafts; other economic and, more important, noneconomic factors must be examined more fully in order to explain the process of handicraft displacement in the Chinese economy.

Manchurian Industrialization

The second qualification concerns the possible upward biases in the rates of industrial growth for China resulting from the inclusion of highly industrialized Manchuria. Before 1931, the pace and pattern of industrial development was not markedly different in China proper from that in Manchuria. After 1931, however, and in the subsequent decade or so, Manchuria experienced a period of rapid expansion due mainly to Japanese capital and management. The growth in the heavy industries, *i.e.*, coal, iron and steel, and electric power, in particular, was remarkable.

The data presented in Table 27 do not represent the results of a systematic study of Manchurian economic development or industrialization—a separate topic which would require special attention. This study is confined to a more limited task —namely, a quantitative assessment of Manchuria's contributions and the corresponding separation of industrial growth in China proper for three benchmark years, 1926, 1931, and 1936. In this connection, it should be noted that Manchuria does not produce several of the mining products listed in the table. To provide a common basis for comparison, the same set of 1933 net value-added weights used earlier in the study was also applied to these benchmark output series for both China proper and Manchuria. The value series on which the growth rates are based are tabulated in Table 28.

The combined growth rate for China proper and Manchuria, as shown in Table 19 above, was 8.3 per cent per year for 1926–36 and 9.3 per cent per year for 1931–36. During the same two periods, the growth rates for China proper were 6.4 per cent and 6.7 per cent, respectively, while for Manchuria they were 14.2 per cent and 16.7 per cent, respectively. These results may not be at all surprising, since they are completely in line with *a priori* expectations.

Closer examination of the 15 series included suggests that the Manchurian growth rates may be biased upward by four of the strategically important industries included in the benchmark index: coal, steel, crude oil, and electric power. It should be noted in particular that both steel and crude oil started with an extremely low base in 1926, and Manchuria did not really start producing steel on a large scale until about 1935. In other words, we may speculate that if some of the consumer goods industries, which expanded at considerably lower rates during this period, were included in the index for Manchuria, the overall rates of growth would be lower than those shown by the benchmark index.[15] Cotton yarn output, for example, which is included in the benchmark index, only slightly more than doubled, while pig iron quadrupled during the ten-year period. It may also be true that the food and beverage and other industries expanded relatively slowly.

15. This speculation can be supported by the results of a recent study by Kungtu C. Sun (1969). According to Sun, the growth rate of the gross value of industrial production, in constant prices, in South and North Manchuria during the period 1926–36 was a meager 4.7 per cent per year (p. 99). The annual growth rate of value-added in industrial production in the Kwantung Leased Territory and the South Manchuria Railway Zone was 7.3 per cent (p. 96).

TABLE 27
INDUSTRIAL PRODUCTION OF CHINA PROPER AND MANCHURIA, PHYSICAL VOLUMES OF OUTPUT

Commodity	Units	1926		1931		1936	
		China proper	Manchuria	China proper	Manchuria	China proper	Manchuria
Coal	1,000 m.t.	10,231	5,437	13,879	7,099	23,648	10,270
Iron ore	,,	294	737	1,084	762	1,241	1,682
Pig iron	,,	117	111	94	250	147	525
Steel	,,	30	*	15	*	70	344
Antimony	,,	20	0	14	0	16	0
Copper	m.t.	156	74	296	117	294	*
Gold	1,000 taels	104	45	64	65	117	84
Mercury	m.t.	100	0	23	0	85	0
Tin	1,000 m.t.	10	0	9	0	13	0
Tungsten	,,	8	0	7	0	10	0
Cotton yarn	1,000 bales	1,926	48	2,284	76	2,039	109
Cotton cloth	1,000 bolts	3,398	366	20,234	2,774	30,479	4,969
Cement	1,000 m.t.	388	108	525	162	663	580
Crude oil	1,000 barrels	2	11	3	450	2	1,286
Electric power	million KWH	456	295	744	543	1,724	1,351

* negligible
Sources and Notes:
    Coal:
    1926 and 1931. Total output, by both modern and traditional methods, for China proper (hereafter CP) and Manchuria (hereafter M), Geological Survey of China (hereafter G.S.), (No. 5, pp. 34–35). Percentage of output by modern method found in Yen Chung-p'ing *et al.,* (1955, p. 104), applied to the total output figures.

1936. Output for CP is the difference between the national total (Yen, p. 103) and M (South Manchuria Railway, 1938, *Manshū keizai nempō*, Table 1).

Iron ore:
All years. China totals, Yen (p. 103); M separated out, South Manchuria Railway (1935, 1936, p. 153). Percentage of output by modern method applied (Yen, p. 104).

Pig iron:
All years. China totals, Yen (p. 103); M separated out, *The Orient Yearbook, 1942* (pp. 603 and 607). Percentage of output by modern method applied (Yen, p. 104).

Steel:
1926 and 1931. M output negligible, Yen (p. 142).
1936. China total, Yen (p. 142); M separated out, Wang Ch'eng-ching (1947, p. 101).

Antimony:
All years. Yen (pp. 139–40).

Copper:
1926 and 1931. National totals, Kuomintang (1937, p. 78); M for 1926, Manchurian Daily News Bureau (1937, p. 328). Manchurian copper ore contained only 15% cu; adjustment made, G.S. (No. 4, p. 153); M for 1931, G.S. (No. 4, p. 153).
1936. CP, G.S. (No. 7, p. 5).

Gold:
1926. China total, Kuomintang (1937, p. 77); M separated out, Manchurian Daily News Bureau (1937, p. 328).
1931. Both CP and M, G.S. (No. 5, p. 5).
1936. Both CP and M, G.S. (No. 7, p. 7).

Mercury:
All years. Yen (p. 140).

Tin:
All years. Yen (p. 140).

Tungsten:
All years. Yen (p. 140).

Cotton yarn:
1926. China total is the author's estimate (see Appendix A for details); M separated out, Kai-zo-sha (1932, p. 496).
1931 and 1936. CP, Yen (p. 130); M, Manshikai (1964, Vol. 2, p. 434).

Cotton cloth:
1926. China total is the author's estimate (see Appendix A for details); M separated out, South Manchuria Railway (1931, p. 27).

(continued)

(Table 27 continued)

1931. CP, Yen (p. 130); M, South Manchuria Railway, *Manshū keizai teiyō,* (1938, p. 397).
1936. CP, Yen (p. 130); M is the author's estimate (see Appendix A for details).

Cement:

1926. China total, *Shen-pao nien-chien* (1936, p. I 82); M separated out, Onoda Company's output only. See South Manchuria Railway, (1930, p. 27).
1931. China total, *Shen-pao nien-chien* (1936, p. I 82); M separated out, *The Orient Year Book, 1942* (p. 686).
1936. CP, G.S. (No. 7, p. 6); M, *The Orient Year Book, 1942* (p. 686).

Crude oil:

1926. CP and M, G.S. (No. 4, p. 113).
1931. CP and M, G.S. (No. 5, pp. 158–59).
1936. CP and M, G.S. (No. 7, p. 85).

Electric power:

1926 and 1931. China total, *The China Annual, 1944* (1945, p. 945); M separated out, *Manshikai* (Vol. II, p. 537).
1936. CP, Chang Tzu-k'ai (1954, pp. 165–171); M, *Manshikai* (Vol. II, p. 537).

TABLE 28
INDUSTRIAL PRODUCTION OF CHINA PROPER AND MANCHURIA,
NET VALUE-ADDED

(millions of 1933 yuan)

Commodity	CHINA PROPER			MANCHURIA		
	1926	1931	1936	1926	1931	1936
Coal	35.8	48.6	82.8	19.0	24.8	35.9
Iron ore	0.8	3.1	3.6	2.1	2.2	4.9
Pig iron	3.1	2.5	3.9	2.9	6.6	13.8
Steel	1.2	0.6	2.8	*	*	13.8
Antimony	2.8	2.0	2.2	*	*	*
Copper	*	0.1	0.1	*	*	*
Gold	7.8	4.8	8.8	3.4	4.9	6.3
Mercury	0.3	0.1	0.3	*	*	*
Tin	17.5	14.8	21.6	*	*	*
Tungsten	3.3	2.7	4.0	*	*	*
Cotton yarn	83.2	98.7	88.1	2.1	3.3	4.7
Cotton cloth	5.8	34.4	51.8	0.6	4.7	8.4
Cement	5.2	7.0	8.8	1.4	2.2	7.7
Crude oil	*	*	*	0.1	5.4	15.4
Electric power	16.4	26.8	62.1	10.6	19.5	48.6
Total	183.2	246.2	340.9	42.2	73.6	159.5
Index	100.0	134.4	186.1	100.0	174.4	378.0

* Less than 0.1 million yuan.

On the other hand, despite the fact that rates for China proper during 1926–36 were considerably lower than the corresponding rates for Manchuria, the growth rates for some of the individual industries in China proper—coal and electric power in particular—compared reasonably well with those in Manchuria.

CHAPTER SIX

China's Industrialization—
Further Observations

ON THE BASIS of the information presented in the foregoing chapters, and the index number series (Table 14) in particular, it may be concluded that pre-Communist China experienced rapid industrial growth, at least in the modern sector. Within the limitations imposed by the scarcity and unreliability of the data, certain characteristics of China's industrialization will be examined. Some additional indicators of industrialization will be discussed.

OTHER INDICATORS OF INDUSTRIALIZATION

The conclusion that pre-Communist China experienced rapid industrial growth seems to be confirmed and even strengthened by certain production-capacity or factory-equipment indicators. For some industries there are no long-term output data, but certain fairly unambiguous measures of production capacity are available, and they can be used as indicators of the growth tendencies in the industries concerned.

The number of cotton yarn spindles and factory looms increased rapidly between 1912 and 1936. (See Table 29.) Spindleage trebled during the 1912–22 period and more than doubled from 1922 to 1936. The loomage figures show even higher rates of expansion, due partly to the low base in 1912. This equipment data substantiates our conclusion that the cotton-spinning industries reached their pre-Communist peak output level during the 1930's. Loomage reached its peak in 1949, but this may represent an unknown amount of idle capacity in 1949, since the peak of cloth output was reached in 1947, according to the series compiled for this study. At any rate, that the industry experienced rapid growth during the prewar period is not to be disputed.

TABLE 29
FACTORY SPINDLES AND LOOMS IN CHINA, 1912–49
(1,000 units)

Year	Spindles	Looms
1912	738	2
1918	1,035	6
1922	2,387	12
1930	4,102	32
1936	5,102	58
1949	4,996	127

Sources:
1912–36, Yen Chung-p'ing *et al.*, 1955 (pp. 134–35).
1949, State Statistical Bureau, 1958 (p. 154).

Flour milling is one of the most important consumer goods industries omitted from this study. Table 30 summarizes the estimates of output capacities in the flour-milling industry

between 1911 and 1949. According to these estimates, productive capacity increased steadily during the period under review.
However, the descriptive literature suggests that this growth in
output reached a peak in 1920 and stagnated throughout the
1920's. This may reflect either inaccuracies in these estimates,

TABLE 30
OUTPUT CAPACITY OF FLOUR, 1911–49

(1,000 bags)

Year	Daily output capacity
1911	47
1914	92
1917	110
1920	117
1923	220
1930	251
1933	326
1949	335

Source:
Huang Chih-ch'iu, 1950 (p. 3).

or the accumulation of idle capacity in the industry, or some
combination of the two.

Another indicator of industrialization is the widespread
development and adoption of modern methods of production,
methods that result not only in increased per capita product
but, more fundamentally, in a higher rate of growth of
productive efficiency. (Cf. Kuznets, 1966, esp. pp. 491–92.)
From this technological point of view, changes in the method
of production from hand-operated to power-driven equipment
and in the modes of organization from small to large establishments would characterize the process of industrialization in an
economy. Data on these changes in the Chinese case are
relatively abundant for the mining sector. The percentages of

total output extracted by mechanized or modern methods in the production of coal, iron ore, and pig iron have been presented in Table 25. These figures clearly demonstrate the trend and extent of mechanization in these three areas, and they show that this process was continuous. By 1949, practically 100 per cent of the output of these products was extracted by mechanized operations. The output by native or traditional methods made only negligible contributions.

Mechanization in the cotton cloth industry was discussed in chapter 5; there are no adequate long-term mechanization data for other manufacturing industries. However, the trend of mechanization in the manufacturing industries may be reflected by the machinery imports into China during the prewar period. Table 31 shows that the value of machinery imports increased almost tenfold between 1912 and 1921, a period of rapid industrial growth. Some of this increase, however, necessarily reflects price changes.[1]

The degree of industrialization of an economy may also be reflected in the export share of certain domestically produced mineral products. In China, the production of a number of important strategic numerals was exclusively for the export trade. The leading item among these minerals was tungsten ore. As an economy industrializes, one would expect that the domestic demand for certain mineral products would increase, with a corresponding percentage reduction in exports. Unfortunately, this indicator is not conclusive for China. Table 32 presents a partial view of the situation.

Another indicator of industrialization of an economy should be the composition of its national income and product (Kuznets, 1966, esp. pp. 113 ff. and 492 ff.). For lack of data, we can observe the behavior of this indicator for only a brief span of time, *i.e.*, from 1931 to 1936. Even for this short period,

1. For example, import prices in Shanghai increased about 42 per cent between 1926 and 1936. (See Chung-kuo k'o-hsüeh yuan, 1958, p. 61.)

TABLE 31
VALUE OF MACHINERY IMPORTS INTO CHINA, 1912–36

(millions of taels)

Year	Value
1912	5.9
1916	6.5
1919	15.3
1921	57.3
1926	19.7
1930	47.5
1936	53.9

Source:
Yang Ta-chin, 1938 (pp. 863–64).

TABLE 32
EXPORTS OF IRON AND TUNGSTEN ORES AS PER CENT
OF TOTAL OUTPUT, 1912–36

Year	Iron ore (per cent)	Tungsten ore (per cent)
1912	93	n.a.
1915	51	n.a.
1918	36	96
1921	50	32
1924	67	51
1927	42	59
1930	48	127
1933	31	96
1936	44	72

Source:
Yen Chung-p'ing et al., 1955 (pp. 139–40).

the national income data were estimated with unknown margins of error, and the estimates made by Ou Pao-san were revised on a number of occasions. Nevertheless, the contribution made by the industrial sector to national income showed a small but consistent increase during this period.

TABLE 33

CONTRIBUTION OF INDUSTRIAL PRODUCTION
TO NATIONAL PRODUCT, 1931–36

(billions of 1933 yuan)

Year	National product		Industrial production		Per cent of national product	
	Ou^a	Yeh^b	Ou^c	Yeh^d	Ou	Yeh
1931	20.35	28.60	0.47	0.87	2.3	3.0
1932	19.97	29.65	0.48	0.94	2.4	3.2
1933	20.01	29.43	0.54	0.97	2.7	3.3
1934	19.10	26.85	0.54	1.03	2.8	3.8
1935	19.44	29.08	0.55	1.14	2.8	3.9
1936	21.37	30.80	0.60	1.28	2.8	4.2

Notes:
   a. "National product," including handicrafts.
   b. "Net domestic product," including handicrafts.
   c. Including mining, metallurgy, and manufacturing. Figures represent 28% of the total value of production, including handicrafts. See Table 24 in chapter 5 of this study for explanation.
   d. Including manufacturing, mining, and utilities; handicrafts excluded.
Sources:
   Ou Pao-san, 1949 (p. 204).
   Yeh Kung-chia, 1964 (p. 225).

On the basis of these estimates, the value of total industrial production, including handicrafts (according to Ou Pao-san's original estimates), accounted for about 10 per cent of China's national product in the 1930's. The contribution made to the national product by the modern industrial sector, handicrafts excluded, was only about 3 per cent in 1933. There are no national income data for the 1940's, when the level of industrial production reached its pre-Communist peak. As a close substitute for China's pre-1949 peak industrial production, the 1952 figure was used. According to Liu and Yeh (1965, Table 8, p. 66), the total net value-added in modern factories, mining, and utilities contributed only 3.4 per cent to the net domestic product in 1933, and it increased to 6.2 per cent in

1952, both valued in terms of constant 1933 prices. Therefore, even in the absence of national income statistics for the pre-1949 peak years, it is safe to conclude that China's modern industrial sector expanded relatively more quickly than the national product, at least up until the early 1940's.

Finally, the degree of industrial development may be positively correlated with the growth or railroad building and the expansion of the railroad industry in general. Table 34

TABLE 34
GROWTH OF RAILROAD MILEAGE, 1912–48
(kilometers)

Period	Total Length	Constructed during period
1912–27	12,040	3,422
1928–31	14,239	1,198
1932–37	21,036	6,797
1938–48	24,945	3,909

Source:
Yen Chung-p'ing *et al.*, 1955 (p. 180).

TABLE 35
INDEXES OF GROWTH OF RAILROAD EQUIPMENT, 1912–47
(1912 = 100)

Year	Locomotives	Passenger cars	Freight cars
1912	100.0	100.0	100.0
1922	165.3	130.7	173.6
1932	197.0	177.6	188.0
1936	207.2	191.8	185.7
1937	166.7	187.4	180.0
1940	63.0	92.9	72.5
1947	325.7	254.5	313.9

Source:
Yen Chung-p'ing *et al.*, 1955 (pp. 194–95).

indicates that railroad mileage increased most rapidly during 1932–37. However, this was mostly in Manchuria. The increase of railroad equipment is shown in Table 35. The increase in total railroad ton-mileage, as well as the indexes of tonnage of various types of goods shipped by railroad, are presented in Table 36. It is important to note that the tonnage of manufacturing and mining products shipped by railroad increased substantially faster than that of agricultural products, especially during the prewar period. This, too, would suggest that the manufacturing and mining sectors expanded relatively more rapidly than did the agricultural sector of the economy.[2]

TABLE 36
INDEXES OF GROWTH OF RAILROAD TRANSPORTATION,
1917–46

(1917 = 100)

Year	Tonnage of manufactured goods	Tonnage of mining products	Tonnage of agricultural products
1917	100.0	100.0	100.0
1925	152.5	132.6	97.0
1933	200.9	192.4	94.6
1936	268.3	282.6	132.9
1937	79.0	111.9	37.5
1942	8.7	10.0	6.1
1946	83.2	80.0	54.3

Source:
Yen Chung-p'ing *et al.*, 1955 (p. 217).

2. For a discussion on the indicators of economic modernization, with particular reference to the contributions made by foreign investment in China, see Hou Chi-ming, 1965, ch. 6. In addition, of course, there are other statistically testable indicators of industrialization, including, for example, the increase of income per capita and the resulting or accompanying changes in composition of production and pattern of demand; but because of the lack of adequate data, no attempt at using such indicators can be made here.

CONCLUDING REMARKS

This study has been largely quantitative in scope. An important part of the record of industrial production in pre-Communist China has been made more manageable, and a reasonably clear picture, in quantitative terms, of China's industrial development has emerged. This work will serve as a background against which the contemporary economic developments in Communist China may be appraised. It should be emphasized that this work is preliminary in nature. It is hoped that it will stimulate, even provoke, more comprehensive and larger-scale quantitative researches on China's industrial development in the pre-Communist period.

Our index shows that China's modern industrial sector expanded at rapid rates during the prewar period. This conclusion has been further strengthened by the evidence presented in this chapter. The average annual rate of growth of the modern industrial sector was about 8 to 9 per cent for prewar China, including Manchuria. Moreover, the modern industrial sector expanded relatively more rapidly than the national product. In short, the record of industrial growth in prewar China is anything but long-term stagnation.

In the light of this rapid expansion of the modern industrial sector, a hypothetical question can be posed: Could these high rates of growth have been sustained into the 1940's or even the 1950's had they not been interrupted by military hostilities? Even more important, would a continuation of these rates of expansion have led to the transformation of the rest of the Chinese economy? More specifically, did these rapidly expanding industries possess any of the characteristics of a "leading sector," making substantial contributions to the nation's economic growth? Available evidence clearly indicates that the Chinese economy as a whole remained largely undeveloped during the pre-Communist period, despite the

rapid expansion of the modern industrial sector. It is crucial
to ask, therefore, why the impact, if any, of the modern
industrial sector on the rest of the economy was so weak and
the process of diffusion so slow within the Chinese context.

There are, of course, no ready answers to these questions.
But a substantial amount of reliable information suggests
that a firm economic, social, and political foundation for
modern economic transformation was being built during the
prewar decade ending in 1937. It is useful to view this suggestion in a broader historical perspective.

In an article that appeared in 1958, Professor Alexander
Eckstein made the following observation about the history of
China's economic development, with particular reference to
the role of the state:

> ... the state has played a passive to actively negative role *vis-
> à-vis* the economy. The very concept of economic change and
> economic dynamism was alien to such a society with the nexus
> between economic growth and national power and/or welfare
> only very dimly understood, if perceived at all. The function of the
> economy was a largely static one, being charged with the primary
> task of supporting the ruling elite. Therefore, the state assumed
> very few responsibilities in the economy, beyond assuring that it
> would provide a stable, continuing, and adequate source of
> revenue for the imperial household and the gentry-bureau-
> cracy.

The continuing failure of the traditional Chinese state to respond
to the challenge of modernization, the institutional rigidities
permeating the traditional social structure, the incapacity and
unwillingness of the ruling classes to come to terms with change,
their inability to understand the character of the innovating in-
fluences and to follow a policy of enlightened self-interest, have
all served to retard the process of industrialization for so long
that cumulative tensions of such explosive proportions were
generated that they could no longer be contained, while at the
same time perhaps nothing short of such an explosive force could

have broken the shackles of the old order and swept away the barriers to economic growth . . . (Eckstein, 1958).

This observation was made in connection with a theoretical discussion of Alexander Gerschenkron's (1965, esp. ch. 1) scheme for economic development. The author has also been struck by the applicability of Gerschenkron's hypothesis and its implications for China's economic development in the past few decades. In a longer historical perspective, external challenges of various forms built up "tension" in China over the centuries, but the political, social, and institutional obstacles were so formidable that the cumulative "tension" was never translated into a "great spurt." In strictly statistical terms, the real Gerschenkronian "spurt" came only in the 1950's; and the violent Chinese Communist attempts since 1949, especially in the 1950's, could best illustrate the Gerschenkronian tension-spurt relationship. From this particular point of view, the Gerschenkronian scheme is applicable only to the Communist period and not to the pre-Communist period. The rates of industrial growth for 1926–36, or for any other subperiods during the prewar years, were not very high when compared to those for a preceding period, so that the statistical test for a "spurt" would therefore be inconclusive.

However, according to Gerschenkron, "no industrialization seemed possible . . . , as long as certain formidable institutional obstacles . . . remained." One of these "obstacles" is the "absence of political unification" (Gerschenkron, 1965, p. 8). In the closing decades of the last century, a number of government leaders, such as Tseng Kuo-fan, Li Hung-chang, and Tso Tsung-tang, established modern factories to manufacture ammunition and weapons. These efforts were largely a response to external challenges—economic, political, and military—presented by Western powers. Attempts made during the 1860's to the 1890's toward economic modernization or industrialization represented no more than individual efforts and had virtually no government support or sponsorship. Similarly, in 1898, the hundred-day reform movement led by K'ang Yu-wei and Liang Ch'i-ch'ao ended in total failure. In other words, there was no concerted government effort in these areas of endeavor, and at this time the role of the government was extremely insignificant. (Cf. Perkins, 1967, pp. 478–92.)

Under the Nanking Government, the period 1928–36 was unique in China's history. Political unification was achieved, however imperfectly. Peace and order were maintained and greatly strengthened.[3] Statistical data compiled in this study seem to indicate some "spurting" tendencies in the economy. In other words, the suggestion may be hazarded that the 1928–36 experience is an illustration of the Gerschenkronian tension-spurt relationship. During this decade, the necessary foundation was being laid for modern economic transformation. The question remains whether "an explosive force" would have been necessary to "break the shackles of the old order" and to "sweep away the barriers to economic growth," to use the words of Professor Eckstein—if the military hostilities between China and Japan could have been averted. Again, there are no ready answers to these questions. However, these suggestions may indicate the areas of worthwhile research on the economic history of pre-Communist China.

3. Perhaps for the first time in the twentieth century. (Cf., for example, John K. Fairbank, Alexander Eckstein, and L. S. Yang, 1960, p. 26.)

APPENDIX A

Output Series

THIS APPENDIX CONTAINS the output series for the 15 commodities from 1912 to 1949. Output data actually compiled from various sources are presented in Table A–1, and those estimated are tabulated in Table A–2. Both tables are accompanied by detailed explanatory notes and source references. Full citations are given in the References.

A dash(—) in Table A–1 indicates that the missing figure has been estimated and tabulated in Table A–2. Blank spaces in Table A–2 represent output data actually compiled and presented in Table A–1. A single asterisk (*) means that the output was negligible. A double asterisk (**) indicates that no output data were found and no estimates were made.

TABLE A-1
OUTPUT SERIES COMPILED, 1912–49

Year	Coal (1,000 M.T.)	Iron ore (1,000 M.T.)	Pig iron (1,000 M.T.)	Steel (1,000 M.T.)	Antimony (1,000 M.T.)
1912	5,166	221	8	3	16
1913	5,678	460	98	43	16
1914	7,974	505	130	56	27
1915	8,493	596	166	48	22
1916	9,483	629	199	45	20
1917	10,479	640	188	43	33
1918	11,109	999	158	57	17
1919	12,805	1,350	237	35	9
1920	14,131	1,336	259	68	16
1921	13,350	1,010	229	77	13
1922	14,060	859	231	30	15
1923	16,973	1,243	171	30	16
1924	18,525	1,266	190	30	13
1925	17,538	1,019	193	30	18
1926	15,617	1,033	228	30	20
1927	17,694	1,181	258	30	20
1928	17,980	1,475	298	30	20
1929	18,854	2,047	301	20	21
1930	19,892	1,774	376	15	18
1931	21,093	1,840	345	15	14
1932	20,213	1,839	413	20	14
1933	22,075	1,903	471	30	14
1934	25,801	2,135	521	50	16
1935	30,093	2,904	648	257	16
1936	33,794	2,922	670	414	16
1937	31,387	3,410	831	556	15
1938	—	—	—	—	11
1939	—	—	—	—	13
1940	—	—	—	—	8
1941	—	—	—	—	8
1942	—	—	—	—	5
1943	—	—	—	923	*
1944	—	—	—	—	*
1945	—	—	—	—	0
1946	—	—	—	16	1
1947	—	—	—	63	2
1948	—	—	—	44	3
1949	30,984	—	246	158	4

TABLE A–1
OUTPUT SERIES COMPILED, 1912–49 (continued)

Year	Copper (M.T.)	Gold (1,000 tael)	Mercury (M.T.)	Tin (1,000 M.T.)	Tungsten (1,000 M.T.)
1912	878	56	7	10	*
1913	908	67	4	9	*
1914	857	90	41	8	*
1915	720	73	188	9	*
1916	720	71	179	9	*
1917	1,081	60	262	13	1
1918	1,031	—	300	10	10
1919	1,091	16	141	10	6
1920	953	8	83	12	7
1921	758	12	98	7	7
1922	747	12	18	10	8
1923	725	4	25	9	6
1924	735	2	3	8	6
1925	1,114	198	408	10	7
1926	230	149	100	10	8
1927	166	102	74	10	8
1928	350	100	68	8	8
1929	312	83	25	8	10
1930	345	114	41	7	7
1931	413	128	23	9	7
1932	440	106	3	7	2
1933	483	112	26	8	6
1934	471	125	101	8	6
1935	355	145	45	10	15
1936	294	200	85	13	10
1937	372	231	61	13	14
1938	447	269	72	15	14
1939	1,886	301	170	14	12
1940	2,318	329	94	11	9
1941	1,591	331	125	11	12
1942	1,266	323	167	8	12
1943	1,033	80	118	4	9
1944	1,018	100	103	2	3
1945	1,179	100	69	3	0
1946	1,530	150	31	2	2
1947	1,070	107	10	4	6
1948	—	—	—	5	10
1949	2,000	—	—	4	5

TABLE A–1
OUTPUT SERIES COMPILED, 1912–49 (continued)

Year	Cotton yarn (1,000 bales)	Cotton cloth (1,000 bolts)	Cement (1,000 M.T.)	Crude oil (1,000 barrels)	Electric power (million KWH)
1912	267	—	—	*	—
1913	400	—	—	1	—
1914	534	—	—	1	—
1915	625	—	—	1	—
1916	667	—	—	2	—
1917	734	—	—	2	—
1918	800	—	—	1	—
1919	1,100	—	—	1	—
1920	1,333	—	—	1	—
1921	1,500	—	—	1	—
1922	1,006	—	306	1	—
1923	—	—	349	1	—
1924	1,486	—	356	1	—
1925	1,792	—	364	1	—
1926	—	—	496	13	751
1927	2,127	8,999	498	20	772
1928	2,175	13,768	608	24	882
1929	2,298	14,780	755	29	1,017
1930	2,401	16,180	691	364	1,112
1931	2,360	23,013	687	452	1,287
1932	2,424	23,255	621	518	1,788
1933	2,447	28,344	727	637	2,074
1934	2,382	28,831	838	677	2,313
1935	2,137	—	—	1,039	2,653
1936	2,148	—	—	1,217	3,075
1937	—	—	—	1,430	—
1938	—	—	—	2,002	—
1939	—	—	—	2,827	—
1940	—	—	—	4,299	—
1941	—	—	—	4,878	—
1942	—	—	—	6,011	—
1943	—	—	—	2,286	—
1944	—	—	—	1,481	—
1945	—	—	—	1,285	—
1946	1,543	37,210	292	515	3,625
1947	1,974	47,625	749	381	—
1948	1,680	—	550	536	—
1949	1,803	30,178	661	864	4,308

Sources:

Coal:
1912–37. Yen Chung-p'ing *et al.*, 1955 (Table 6, pp. 102–103).
1949. State Statistical Bureau, 1959 (pp. 84–89).

Iron ore:
1912–37. Yen Chung-p'ing *et al.*, 1955 (pp. 102–103).

Pig iron:
1912–37. Yen Chung-p'ing *et al.*, 1955.
1949. Chao Kang, 1965 (Table C–1, p. 121).

Steel:
1912–37. Yen Chung-p'ing *et al.*, 1955 (pp. 141–42).
1943. Helen Yin and Y. C. Yin, 1960 (p. 50).
1946–47. *Chung-hua nien-chien*, 1948 (p. 1569).
1948. United Nations, 1949 (p. 37).
1949. State Statistical Bureau, 1959 (pp. 84–89).

Antimony:
1912–37. Yen *et al.*, 1955 (pp. 139–40).
1938–42. Geological Survey of China (No. 7, p. 5). Data include Free China only, however.
1943–47. *Chung-hua nien-chien*, 1948 (p. 1569).
1948. Wu Yuan-Li, 1956 (p. 296).
1949. U.S. Dept. of Interior, Bureau of Mines, 1960 (p. 10).

Copper:
1912–24. Geological Survey of China (No. 2, pp. 176 ff).
1925–28. Kuomintang, 1937 (p. 78).
1929–37. Geological Survey of China (Nos. 4, 5, and 7).
1938–47. *Chung-hua nien-chien*, 1948 (p. 1569).
1949. U.S. Dept. of Interior, Bureau of Mines, 1960 (p. 10).

Gold:
1912–17. Geological Survey of China, 1919 (p. 55).
1919–24. *The China Year Book, 1926–27* (p. 119).
1925–34. Kuomintang, 1937 (p. 77).
1935–42. Geological Survey of China (No. 7, p. 4).
1943–47. *Chung-hua nien-chien*, 1948 (p. 1569).

Mercury:
1912–37. Yen *et al.*, 1955 (pp. 139–40).
1938–42. Geological Survey of China (No. 7, p. 5).
1943–47. *Chung-hua nien-chien*, 1948 (p. 1569).

Tin:
1912–37. Yen *et al.*, 1955 (pp. 139–40).
1938–42. Geological Survey of China (No. 7, p. 4).
1943–45. T'an Hsi-hung, 1948 (p. K 11).
1946–47. *Chung-hua nien-chien*, 1948 (p. 1569).
1948–49. United Nations, 1949 (p. 34).

Tungsten:
1914–17. Yang Ta-chin, 1938 (Vol. II, p. 435).
1918–37. Yen Chung-p'ing *et al.*, 1955 (pp. 139–40).
1938–42. Geological Survey of China (No. 7, p. 4).

1943–44. T'an Hsi-hung, 1948 (p. K 4).
1945–47. *Chung-hua nien-chien,* 1948 (p. 1569).
1948. Wu Yuan-li, 1956 (p. 29).
1949. U.S. Dept. of Interior, 1960 (p. 10).

Cotton yarn:
1912–13, 1919, and 1921. Hou Hou-p'ei, 1929 (pp. 94–95).
1914, 1916–18. Arno Pearse, 1929 (p. 154).
1915. Great Britain, Economic Missions, 1931 (pp. 54–55).
1920. Chin Rockwood, 1937 (p. 67).
1922, 1924–25, 1927–30. Yen Chung-p'ing *et al.,* 1955 (p. 13).
1931–32 and 1934–36. China proper (Yen *et al.,* p. 130) and Manchuria (Manshikai, Vol. II, p. 434) were aggregated to derive the national totals.
1933. Yin and Yin, 1960 (p. 50).
1946. Directorate General of Budget, Accounts, and Statistics, 1947 (No. 124).
1947. Cheng Yu-k'wei, 1956 (p. 267).
1948. United Nations, 1949 (p. 44).
1949. Yin and Yin, 1960 (p. 50).

Cotton cloth:
1927–30. Yen Chung-p'ing *et al.,* 1955 (p. 130).
1931–34. China proper (Yen *et al.,* 1955) plus Manchuria (South Manchuria Railway, 1938, *Manshū keizai teiyō,* p. 397) to represent the national totals.
1946–47. Cheng Yu-k'wei, 1956 (p. 267).
1949. Yin and Yin, 1960 (p. 50).

Cement:
1922–31. *Shen-pao nien-chien, 1936* (p. 182)
1932–34. China proper *(Shen-pao nien-chien, 1936)* and Manchuria *(The Orient Yearbook, 1942,* p. 686) combined to represent the national totals.
1946. Wang Foh-shen, 1948a (p. 7).
1947–48. United Nations, 1949 (p. 43).
1949. Yin and Yin, 1960 (p. 50).

Crude oil:
By definition used in this study, "crude oil" includes natural petroleum, shale oil, and synthetic oil. Before 1926, the series does not include shale and synthetic oil. The specific source references are as follows:
1912–24. Chao P'ing, 1935 (pp. 24–25).
1925. Kuomintang, 1937 (p. 71).
1926–30. Geological Survey of China (No. 4, p. 113).
1931–34. *Ibid.* (No. 5, p. 158).
1935–42. *Ibid.* (No. 7, p. 85).
1943–48. Chang Tzu-k'ai, 1954 (p. 208); Yin and Yin, 1960 (p. 50); Wu Yuan-li, 1956 (p. 29).
1949. State Statistical Bureau, 1959.

Electric power:
1926–31. *The China Annual,* 1945 (p. 945).
1932–36. Chang Tzu-k'ai, 1954 (pp. 165–171); Manshikai, 1964 (Vol. I,I p. 537). These are the two sources for China proper and Manchuria.
1946. Wang Foh-shen, 1948a.

TABLE A-2
OUTPUT SERIES ESTIMATED, 1912–49ª

Year	Coal (1,000 M.T.)	Iron ore (1,000 M.T.)	Pig iron (1,000 M.T.)	Steel (1,000 M.T.)	Copper (M.T.)	Gold (1,000 taels)	Mercury (M.T.)	Cotton yarn (1,000 bales)	Cotton cloth (1,000 bolts)	Cement (1,000 M.T.)	Electric power (million KWH)
1912									732	90	53
1913									836	81	69
1914									1,087	110	79
1915									1,500	112	95
1916									1,765	105	108
1917									1,628	125	123
1918						38			1,437	133	141
1919									1,840	144	149
1920									1,892	142	161
1921									2,504	161	237
1922									2,190		291
1923								1,246	3,199		443
1924									2,554		576
1925									3,113		706
1926								1,974	3,764		
1927											
1928											
1929											
1930											

Year	Coal (1,000 M.T.)	Iron ore (1,000 M.T.)	Pig iron (1,000 M.T.)	Steel (1,000 M.T.)	Copper (M.T.)	Gold (1,000 taels)	Mercury (M.T.)	Cotton yarn (1,000 bales)	Cotton cloth (1,000 bolts)	Cement (1,000 M.T.)	Electric power (million KWH)
1931											
1932											
1933											
1934											
1935									30,298	1,027	
1936									35,448	1,243	
1937								1,447	25,341	1,072	1,864
1938	28,749	3,030	875	586				717	10,189	1,442	2,327
1939	34,688	4,390	1,071	522				802	13,629	1,318	2,773
1940	44,334	6,813	1,106	534				764	6,767	1,415	3,331
1941	55,423	7,812	1,441	576				848	7,485	1,479	3,889
1942	58,374	9,452	1,713	765				516	7,439	1,912	4,651
1943	50,459	10,170	1,794					500	6,909	1,830	5,220
1944	51,027	7,586	1,340	491				400	4,771	1,442	5,314
1945	26,285	446	213	260				300	3,292	1,170	4,876
1946	16,342	294	29								
1947	17,538	142	34								4,671
1948	12,420	150	40		1,535	76	**		35,561		4,498
1949		560				54	**				

ᵃ No estimates were made for antimony, tin, tungsten, or crude oil.

Sources:

Coal:

1938–48. For this period there are only aggregated output data, including coal production by both the traditional and modernized methods. In 1937, the contribution made by the modern sector to the total was 84% (see Yen Chung-p'ing *et al.*, 1955, p. 104), and by 1949, this percentage was increased to 96 (see Chao Kang, 1965, Table C–1, p. 120). Based on these two estimates of contribution made by the traditional sector, and average trend value of 90% was assumed and applied to the aggregated output figures for this period in order to derive the estimated output series representing the contributions made by the modern sector only. For specific years during this period, see the following sources:

1938–39. Geological Survey of China (No. 7, p. 4).

1940–43. See Ching-chi-pu (1944 and 1945) for data on free China, and see Yen Chung-p'ing *et al.*, (1955, p. 143) for data on the Japanese-occupied areas during the war.

1944. Wu Yuan-li, 1956 (p. 29).

1945. Data for the interior were taken from T'an Hsi-hung, 1948 (pp. 127–28); for data on the Japanese-occupied areas see Yen Chung-p'ing *et al.* (1955, p. 143).

1946–47. Chang Tzu-k'ai, 1954 (pp. 196–97).

1948. United Nations, 1949 (p. 25).

Iron ore:

1938–49. As in the case of coal production, there are only combined output statistics for the modern and traditional sectors for this period. Again, on the basis of available information, it was assumed that the contribution made by the modern sector was, on an average, about 95% during this period. For output statistics for the specific years during the period, the following sources have been consulted:

1938–41. Wu Yuan-li, 1956 (pp. 28–29).

1942–45. The wartime output for these years was represented by the output of the occupied areas (Yen Chung-p'ing *et al.*, 1955, p. 143) and by that of the mines controlled and operated by the National Resource Commission (*Ibid.*, p. 157).

1946. The output for this year was interpolated.

1947–48. United Nations, 1949 (p. 32).

1949. Chao Kang, 1965 (p. 120).

Pig iron:

1938–48. Again, there are no disaggregated output figures for the modern and traditional sectors. On the basis of available information on percentage distribution in 1937 and in 1949, it was assumed that the modern sector's contribution to the total for this period was on an average about 95%. Output statistics for specific years during the period are taken from the following sources:

1938–45. Outputs for the occupied areas (Yen *et al.*, 1955, p. 143) and for Free China (*Chung-hua nien-chien*, 1948, Vol. II, p. 1569) were aggregated to derive the estimated national totals.

1946–47. *Chung-hua nien-chien, loc. cit.*

1948. Output for this year was extrapolated on the assumption that the rate of recovery from 1947 to 1948 was the same as that from 1946 to 1947.

Steel:
1938–42. The national output for these wartime years was represented by the output in Free and North China (see Wang Foh-shen, 1948a, p. 7) and in Manchuria (Manshikai, 1964, Vol. II, pp. 481–83).

1944. The national output for this year was based on regional output of the interior (Ching-chi-pu, 1945, No. 3); North China (Yen Chung-p'ing *et al.*, 1955, pp. 146–47); and Manchuria (Yen, *loc. cit.*).

1945. In 1944, the production of steel in Manchuria was severely interrupted by U.S. bombing; the output was almost halved from 1943 to 1944. Such interruption was continued and intensified in 1945. It was assumed, therefore, that the rate of decline in the production of steel from 1944 to 1945 was about the same as from 1943 to 1944.

Copper:
1948. Interpolated.

Gold:
1918. Interpolated.
1948–49. Extrapolated on the assumption that the rate of decline from 1946 to 1947 was applicable to these two years.

Mercury:
1948–49. No production data were found for these two years. Since the output was negligible, no effort was made to attempt any estimates.

Cotton yarn:
1923. Interpolated.
1926. Mill consumption of cotton in this year was reported to be 6,581,000 *tan* (*Shen-pao nien-chien, 1934*, p. 686). Estimates show that about 10% of the cotton was wasted in the spinning process (see Ou Pao-san, 1947a, Vol. II, p. 90), so that the amount of yarn produced should be about 5,922,900 *tan* (6,581,000 less 10%), which is equivalent to 1,974,000 bales of 400 pounds.

1937. For this year, neither national data nor reasonably complete regional data was found for China proper. It was assumed, therefore, that the reported 35% decline in yarn output of Shanghai factories from 1936 to 1937 (see Economic Research Bureau of Shanghai, 1944, p. 194) was representative of the country, exclusive of Manchuria. The output of yarn in China proper for this year was estimated to be 1,325,000 bales. Manchurian yarn output for 1937 (South Manchuria Railway, 1938, *Manshū keziai nempō*, Table 1) was then combined to derive the estimated national total.

1938–45. For this period, no global output data were found. Regional output figures for Free China, North China, Shanghai, and Manchuria were aggregated to derive the national totals. (For cotton textiles, this aggregation is quite representative of the country as a whole.) Even regional data in this case were not complete, and some of the gaps had been filled by interpolation. The interpolated estimates included 1942 and 1945 of Manchuria, and 1944–45 of Shanghai. Continuous series are available for Free and North China for these war years. The specific sources of data are as follows:

Free and North China: Wang Foh-shen, 1948a (p. 7).

Manchuria:
  1938. South Manchuria Railway, 1942 (Table 2).
  1939–40. Manshikai, 1964 (p. 444).
  1941 and 1943–44. Yen Chung-p'ing *et al.*, 1955 (p. 146).
Shanghai:
  Economic Research Bureau of Shanghai, 1944 (p. 194).

Cotton cloth:
  1912–26. See Chapter 2.
  1935–36. Manchuria's output for these two years were interpolated on the basis of 3,847,750 bales in 1934 (South Manchuria Railway, 1938, *Manchū keizai teiyō*, p. 397) and 5,530,000 bales in 1937 (Yen Chung-p'ing *et al.*, 1955, p. 146). These interpolated estimates for Manchuria were added to China proper's totals (Yen Chung-p'ing *et al*, 1955, p. 130) to derive the national totals.
  1937–39. The output for China proper was estimated on the assumption that the situation of the industry in the Shanghai factories was representative of the rest of the area, exclusive of Manchuria. According to the Economic Research Bureau of Shanghai (1944, No. 1, p. 194), the output of cotton cloth in the Shanghai factories declined from its 1936 level by 35, 84, and 72% in 1937, 1938, and 1939, respectively. Output estimates for these three years were made on the basis of output for China proper in 1936. Manchurian output for 1938 and 1939 was interpolated on the basis of available output information for 1937 and 1941 (Yen Chung-p'ing *et al.*, 1955, p. 146).
  1940–45. Again, the national totals were represented by aggregating regional data for the interior, Shanghai, and Manchuria. But even regional data for these wartime years were extremely scarce, and some of the gaps had been filled by means of interpolation or extrapolation. These included 1940 and 1942 of Manchuria and 1944 of Shanghai. The estimated total for 1945 was extrapolated on the basis of 1943–44 rate of decline. Some of the specific sources are as follows:
Free China:
  Ching-chi-pu, 1944, 1945 (Nos. 2 and 3).
Shanghai:
  Economic Research Bureau of Shanghai, 1944 (No. 1, p. 194).
Manchuria:
  South Manchuria Railway, 1942 (No. 2), and Yen Chung-p'ing *et al.*, 1955 (p. 146).
  1948. Interpolated.

Cement:
  1912–21. No national output data were found for this early period. It was assumed, therefore, that the combined output of the Chinese-owned Ch'i-hsin and the Japanese-owned Onoda (Dairen branch) accounted for the nation's total output. The sources of data are:
  Nankai University Economic Research Bureau, 1963 (p. 151); and South Manchuria Railway, 1930 (pp. 26–27).
  1935–37. The nation's totals are represented by Free China (Geological Survey of China, No. 7) and Manchuria (*The Orient Yearbook, 1942*, p. 686) only.
  1938–40. The nation's totals are represented by Free and North China

(Wang Foh-shen, 1948a) and Manchuria (South Manchuria Railway, 1942, Table 2). The other Japanese-occupied areas during the war were not accounted for.

1941–45. Again, the nation's totals are represented by Free and North China (Wang, 1948a) and Manchuria (Chang Ch'en-ta, 1954, p. 240). The Manchurian output for 1945, however, was extrapolated.

Electric power:
1912–25. The generating capacity data for the Chinese-owned power plants are reported in *Shen-pao nien-chien* (1936, p. 190), from 1912 to 1935. In addition, data on the number of KWH's generated in the Chinese plants during 1923–34 are reported by the same source. Based on these two series, the ratio of the electricity generated to the generating capacity from 1923 to 1934 was calculated. There was continuous and almost even increase in the value of this ratio. In 1923 the ratio was 1.54, and in 1934 it was increased to 2.27. On an average, therefore, the ratio increased by about 0.6 per year. On the basis of this trend value, we have estimated the amounts of electricity generated in the Chinese power plants during 1912–22 by using the available generating capacity data. This gives us, then, a continuous series on electricity generated by the Chinese-owned plants from 1912 to 1934. The output for the period 1912–22 represents the estimates made by the author.

From other sources, there is not only the nation's total electricity output, but also a breakdown between foreign and Chinese plants for the period 1926–36. (For 1926–31, see *Shen-pao nien-chien*, 1936, p. 190; and for 1932–36, see Yen Chung-p'ing *et al.*, 1955, p. 130.) Some idea of the extent of the relative importance of each group can be based on this partial disaggregated information. Over this ten-year period, the Chinese plants gained increasing importance in their contribution to total electricity generated. In 1926, for example, the contribution of Chinese plants was only 27% of the total; but by 1936, it had increased to 45%. On the basis of this trend of development, it was assumed that the contribution made by the Chinese plants to total output during 1919–25 was about 25%, and during 1912–18, about 20%. The nation's electricity output for 1912–25 was then estimated on the basis of these assumptions.

1937. The nation's total was represented by Free China (T'an Hsi-hung, 1948, pp. J 24–25), North China (Yen Chung-p'ing *et al.*, 1955, p. 147), and Manchuria (Manshikai, 1964, Vol. II, p. 537).

1938–44. The nation's totals are represented by Free and North China (Wang, 1948a), and Manchuria (State Statistical Bureau, 1958, p. 40).

1945. Free and North China (Wang, 1948a) and Manchuria (extrapolated) combined.

1947. Chang Tzu-k'ai (1954, pp. 165–71) reported that between January and October of 1947, China generated 3,892,409,000 KWH. This figure was multiplied by 1.2 to derive the total for the year.

1948. Interpolated.

APPENDIX B

Price and Value-Added Data

TABLE B

PRICE AND VALUE-ADDED DATA

(unit: yuan)

Commodity	Unit	1925 Gross price	1933 Gross price	1933 Net value added	1952 Gross price
Coal	ton	8.0[a]	5.0[c]	3.5[c]	12.5[g]
Iron ore	ton	3.0[a]	4.0[c]	2.9[c]	20.0[g]
Pig iron	ton	40.0[a]	51.0[c]	26.3[c]	200.0[g]
Steel	ton	87.0[b]	100.0[c]	40.0[c]	600.0[g]
Antimony	ton	400.0[a]	201.0[c]	140.7[c]	2,530.0[g]
Copper	ton	670.0[a]	585.0[c]	316.8[c]	2,530.0[g]
Gold	tael	35.0[a]	100.0[c]	75.0[c]	95.0[g]
Mercury	ton	3,100.0[a]	3,212.0[c]	3,212.0[c]	7,516.0[g]
Tin	ton	2,100.0[a]	2,327.0[c]	1,689.0[c]	3,200.0[g]
Tungsten	ton	300.0[a]	544.0[c]	408.0[c]	1,273.0[g]
Cotton yarn	bale	260.0[b]	182.0[d]	43.2[f]	720.0[d]
Cotton cloth	bolt	11.8[b]	7.7[d]	1.7[f]	27.0[d]
Cement	barrel	4.0[a]	6.0[c]	2.5[c]	14.5[d]
Crude oil	barrel	4.0[a]	20.0[c]	12.0[c]	160.0[g]
Electric power	1,000 KWH	—	60.0[e]	35.9[e]	—

— Not available.

Sources:
  a). Kuomintang, 1937.
  b). Chung-kuo k'o-hsüeh yüan, Shang-hai ching-chi yen-chiu-so, 1958.
  c). Ou Pao-san *et al.*, 1947a (pp. 53–54).
  d). Liu Ta-chung and Yeh Kung-chia, 1965 (p. 449).
  e). Liu and Yeh, 1965 (p. 578).
  f). See Note 4 below.
  g). Liu and Yeh, 1965 (p. 569).

Notes:
  1. Source a contains no explanation concerning the nature of the price data. But the price data for 1933 contained in the same source agree, in most cases, with those found in Ou Pao-san, source c. Since Ou's prices are f.o.b. factory prices, it was assumed that those found in source a were of the same kind.
  2. Source b shows Shanghai retail prices.
  3. Liu and Yeh depended almost entirely upon Ou Pao-san for their 1933 price data.
  4. 1933 net value-added data, for most items, are directly derived from Ou's data, source c. For cotton yarn and cotton cloth, however, it was necessary to make our own estimates. In Liu and Yeh (1965, p. 448) there are gross value-added data for these two items. From various other sources we have obtained estimates of depreciation costs with which the net value-added estimates for cotton yarn and cotton cloth have been derived. The following table summarizes the estimating results:

Item	Unit price	Estimated[a] gross value added per unit	Depreciation cost per unit	Estimated net value added per unit
Cotton yarn	$182.0	$46.9	$3.7[b]	$43.2
Cotton cloth	7.7	1.8	0.1[c]	1.7

Notes:
  a). Based on the ratio between total gross value-added and total gross value of output for each commodity (Liu and Yeh, 1965, p. 448).
  b). An estimate of $3.74/bale of 20-count yarn was found in Wang Tzu-chien and Wang Chen-chung, 1935 (p. 204). In Ou Pao-san (1947a, Vol. II, p. 95) the depreciation cost per bale of 20-count yarn was estimated at 2% of unit price, or $3.64 (2% of $182), in this case. The two sources agreed almost perfectly on this cost estimate.
  c). An estimate of 1% of gross value output was given in Ou Pao-san, 1947a (Vol. II, p. 98)—about $0.10 in this case.

Indexes of Industrial Production: 14 Series

FOR COMPARATIVE PURPOSES we present in Table C a set of three indexes weighted by 1925, 1933, and 1952 unit gross prices. These indexes are less complete in product coverage[1] than the first set presented in chapter 4. It was hoped that by using different price weights we could observe different patterns and rates of growth over the period concerned. But, as shown in Table C, price weights of different years have yielded virtually no discrepancies among the three index numbers before 1936.[2] During the wartime years, however,

---

1. The electric power series is omitted for lack of appropriate price data.

2. In the early stages of economic development, some commodities are produced in small quantities and sold at high prices. At a later stage, the quantities produced will be greater, and the prices lower, because of the application of new technology and other factors. In view of this, one would normally expect that the indexes based on earlier year weights would produce higher rates of growth than those based on later year weights. It should be pointed out here that the findings of this study do not conform to this hypothesis, which is discussed extensively in the literature on index numbers.

TABLE C
INDUSTRIAL PRODUCTION OF MAINLAND CHINA, 1912–49
(14 commodities)

Year	1925 YUAN Millions	Index 1933 = 100	1933 YUAN Millions	Index 1933 = 100	1952 YUAN Millions	Index 1933 = 100
1912	151.8	12.4	116.4	13.2	370.4	11.6
1913	198.8	16.3	153.4	17.3	521.2	16.3
1914	261.1	21.4	197.2	22.4	698.0	21.8
1915	294.3	24.1	220.6	25.0	773.6	24.2
1916	315.7	25.8	235.0	26.6	822.0	25.7
1917	353.8	29.0	263.5	29.9	927.2	29.0
1918	364.2	29.8	271.1	30.7	945.0	29.6
1919	457.3	37.4	334.3	37.9	1,175.6	36.8
1920	540.7	44.3	395.0	44.8	1,409.4	44.1
1921	572.3	46.8	412.9	46.8	1,508.7	47.2
1922	451.1	36.9	330.7	37.5	1,146.7	35.9
1923	545.8	44.7	392.3	44.5	1,381.3	43.2
1924	610.8	50.0	437.2	49.6	1,816.9	56.9
1925	720.1	57.5	518.1	58.7	1,808.3	56.6
1926	745.9	61.0	549.2	62.3	1,952.8	61.1
1937	862.8	70.6	623.8	70.7	2,234.1	69.9
1928	934.3	76.5	672.7	76.3	2,418.1	75.7
1929	989.5	81.0	712.7	80.8	2,565.1	80.3
1930	1,041.1	85.2	754.4	85.5	2,735.3	85.6
1931	1,121.9	91.8	809.7	91.8	2,910.9	91.1
1932	1,131.1	92.6	814.2	92.3	2,940.4	92.1
1933	1,221.8	100.0	882.0	100.0	3,194.0	100.0
1934	1,248.4	102.2	908.7	103.0	3,255.3	101.9
1935	1,276.6	104.5	945.0	107.2	3,424.7	107.2
1936	1,391.6	113.9	1,042.9	118.2	3,770.9	118.1
1937	1,092.6	89.4	854.3	96.8	3,118.7	97.6
1938	721.2	59.0	627.2	71.0	2,291.2	71.7
1939	838.7	68.6	721.4	81.6	2,672.9	83.8
1940	1,023.7	83.8	747.3	84.6	2,865.2	89.7
1941	978.2	80.1	865.4	97.9	3,299.3	103.3
1942	951.9	77.9	885.3	100.2	3,490.7	109.3
1943	862.7	70.6	750.1	84.9	2,840.0	88.9
1944	733.3	60.0	603.4	68.3	2,140.1	67.0
1945	401.0	32.8	331.7	37.5	1,303.6	40.8
1946	994.3	81.4	695.1	78.6	2,476.0	77.5

continued

TABLE C continued

Year	1925 YUAN		1933 YUAN		1952 YUAN	
	Millions	Index 1933 = 100	Millions	Index 1933 = 100	Millions	Index 1933 = 100
1974	1,255.5	102.8	878.2	99.4	3,130.4	98.0
1948	993.8	81.3	703.2	79.6	2,538.9	79.5
1949	1,130.9	92.6	804.4	91.0	2,885.3	90.3

Sources:
Appendixes A and B.

changes in weight bases do show some divergence. The 1925 price structure (see Appendix B for detailed price information), as compared with those for 1933 and for 1952, gives relatively more weight to the consumer products. Prices of crude oil, iron ore, pig iron, steel, and some other mineral products for 1925 were below those of 1933. On the other hand, 1925 prices for cotton yarn and cotton cloth exceeded those for 1933 by a considerable margin. This 1925 price structure, coupled with the fact that the consumer goods industries included in the indexes suffered substantial declines during the war years, accounts in large part for the fact that the 1925-weighted gross output index falls far below those weighted by 1933 or 1952 prices. The same reasoning could also be used to explain, partially at least, the divergence between the 1933-weighted and the 1952-weighted indexes during the war years. Differences in price structure for the two groups of commodities cited are less marked in the 1933–52 comparison than in the 1925–33 case.

On the basis of the foregoing, it would seem that movements in the consumer goods industries exerted a controlling effect on the behavior of these indexes. From the viewpoint of index-making theory, this aspect may be undesirable, since the composite index should not be overwhelmingly influenced

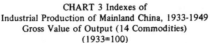

CHART 3 Indexes of
Industrial Production of Mainland China, 1933-1949
Gross Value of Output (14 Commodities)
(1933=100)

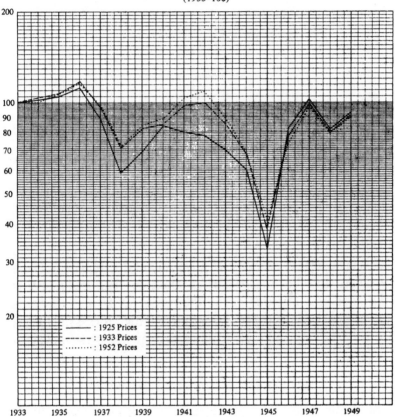

by the activities of a small number of series.[3] However, the
fact remains that Mainland China's modern industrial sector
was indeed dominated by a small number of industries before
the war.

3. See, for example, United Nations, 1961 (p. 34).

References

This is an alphabetical list of government documents, journal articles, and books specifically cited in this study and is designed as a research aid to the reader. It does not include other works consulted by the author and therefore is not meant to be a bibliography on China's prewar industrial development.

PART I: CHINESE AND JAPANESE

Central Bank of China, Economic Research Department, 1939, 1946, 1948. *Chung-yang yin-hang yüeh-pao* (*Central Bank Monthly*), Vol. 8, No. 12 (December, 1939); New Series Vol. 1, No. 1 (January, 1946); Vol. 1, No. 6 (June, 1946); and Vol. 3, No. 12 (December, 1948).

CHANG CH'EN-TA, 1954. *Tung-pei ching-chi* (*The Economy of Manchuria*), Vols. 1 and 2. Taipei.

CHANG TZU-K'AI, 1954 (Ed.). *Chung-kuo kung-yeh* (*China's industries*). Taipei.

CHANG YUNG-HUI and CHANG HSI-NIEN, 1942. *San-shih nien lai chih Chung-kuo tsao-chih kung-yeh* (*China's Paper Industry during the past 30 years*). Research Bulletin No. 120, Central Industrial Testing Center, Ministry of Economic Affairs. Chungking.

CHAO CHANG-FU, April 1943. "Wo-kuo kung-k'uang t'ung-chi chih hui-ku yü ch'ien-chan" ("A Review of and the Prospects for China's Industrial Statistics"), *Ching-chi chien-she chi-k'an* (*Economic Reconstruction Quarterly*), Vol. 1, No. 4. pp. 271–275.

CHAO P'ING, 1935. "Chung-kuo shih-yu-yeh kai-shu" "The Petroleum Industry of China", *Kung-shan pan-yüeh k'an* (*Semi-Monthly Economic Journal*), Vol. 7, No. 9, pp. 24–25.

CHAO TS'UNG, 1935. "Tsui chin wo-kuo chih hou-ch'ai yeh" ("Recent Development in the Chinese Match Industry"), *Kung-shang pan-yüeh k'an* (*Semi-Monthly Economic Journal*), Vol. 7, No. 3 (February, 1935).

Ching-chi-pu (Ministry of Economic Affairs), 1943. *Hou-fang kung-yeh kai-k'uang t'ung-chi* (*Industrial Statistics of the Wartime Interior*). Chungking.

Ching-chi-pu (Ministry of Economic Affairs), 1944, 1945. *Hou-fang chung-yao kung-k'uang ch'an-p'in t'ung-chi* (*Production Statistics of Principal Industrial and Mineral Products in the Wartime Interior*), Nos. 2 and 3. Chungking.

CHOU HSIU-LÜAN, 1958. *Ti-i-tz'u shih-chieh ta-chan shih-ch'i Chung-kuo min-tsu kung-yeh ti fa-chan* (*Industrial Development in China during the First World War*). Shanghai.

Chung-hua nien-chien (*Chung-hua Yearbook*), 1948. Shanghai.

"Chung-kuo chih-yeh tiao-ch'a pao-kao" ("Survey Report of China's Paper Industry"), *Ching-chi yen-chiu* (*Economic Research*), Vol. 1, Nos. 7 and 8 (March and April, 1940).

Chung-kuo ching-chi nien-chien, 1947 (Chinese Economic Yearbook, 1947), The Pacific Economic Research Bureau, Hong Kong.

Chung-kuo k'o-hsüeh yuan (Chinese Academy of Sciences), 1958. *Nan-yang hsiung-ti yen-t'sao kung-ssu shih-liao* (*Historical*

Documents on Nanyang Brothers Tobacco Company). Shanghai.

Chung-kuo k'o-hsüeh yuan, ching-chi yen-chiu-so, 1957. (The Chinese Academy of Sciences, Economic Research Bureau), *1954-nien ch'uan-kuo ko-t'i shou-kung-yeh tiao-ch'a tzŭ-liao* (*1954 Survey of China's Individual Handicrafts*). Peking.

Chung-kuo k'o-hsüeh yuan, Shang-hai ching-chi yen chiu-so (Shanghai Economic Research Bureau, The Chinese Academy of Sciences), 1958 *Shang-hai chieh-fang ch'ien-hou wu-chia tzŭ-liao hui-pien* (*A Compendium on Shanghai Commodity Prices before and after the Liberation*). Shanghai.

Chung-kuo nien-chien, ti-i-hui, 1924. (*China Yearbook, No. 1*). Shanghai.

Directorate General of Budget, Accounts, and Statistics, 1947. *T'ung-chi yüeh pao* (*Statistical Monthly*), Nos. 123 and 124. Nanking.

Economic Research Bureau of Shanghai, 1944. *Shang-hai chan-shih ching-chi* (*Wartime Economy of Shanghai*), No. 1. Shanghai.

Fang Hsien-t'ing (H. D. Fong), 1934. *Chung-kuo chih mien-fang-chih yeh* (*China's Cotton Textiles*). Shanghai.

Fang Hsien-t'ing (H. D. Fong) and Ku Yüan-t'ien, 1934. *Chung-kuo chih kung-yeh chiang-i ta-kang* (*A Lecture Outline of China's Industries*). Tientsin.

Geological Survey of China, 1919. *Chung-kuo k'uang-ch'an chih-lüeh* (*Summary Statement on Chinese Mining*). Peking.

Hou Hou-p'ei, 1929. *Chung-kuo chin-tai ching-chi fa-chan shih* (*History of Economic Development of Modern China*). Shanghai.

Hsü Wu, 1934. "Chung-kuo chih-yeh sheng-ch'an t'ung-chi" ("Output Statistics of China's Paper Industry"), *Shih-yeh t'ung-chi* (*Industrial Statistics*), Vol. 2, No. 6 (December, 1934).

Huang Chih-ch'iu, "Wo-kuo mien-fen kung-yeh ti hui-ku yü chan-wang" ("The Past and Future of China's Flour-Milling Industries"), *Chung-kuo kung-yeh* (*China's Industries*), Vol. 2, No. 6 (October, 1950).

KAI-ZO-SHA, 1932. *Mammō jijō sōran* (*Manchurian and Mongolian Affairs*). Tokyo.

KUNG CHÜN, 1933. *Chung-kuo hsin kung-yeh fa-chan shih ta-kang* (*Outline History of the Development of Modern Industry in China*). Shanghai.

Kuomintang, Ching-chi chi-hua wei-yuan-hui (Economic Planning Commission), 1937. *Shih-nien lai chih Chung-kuo ching-chi chien-she* (*Economic Reconstruction of China during the Past Ten Years*). Nanking.

LIU TA-CHÜN (D. K. Lieu), 1937. *Chung-kuo kung-yeh tiao-ch'a pao-kao* (*Report on a Survey of Chinese Industries*), 3 Vols. Nanking.

Manchurian Daily News Bureau, 1937. *Manshū nenkan* (*Manchurian Yearbook*). Dairen.

Manshikai (Association for Manchurian History), 1964. *Manshū kaihatsu yonjūnen shi* (*A Forty-Year History of Manchurian Development*), 3 Vols. Tokyo.

Mow Sing and Foh Sing Flour Mills and Sung Sing Cotton Mills, 1929.*Mao-hsin Fu-hsin Shen-hsin tsung-kung-ssu sa-chou-nien chi-nien ts'e* (The *30th Annniversary Memorial book, 1898–1928*). Shanghai.

Nankai ta-hsüeh, Tientsin ching-chi yen-chiu-so, (Nankai University, Economic Research Bureau of Tientsin), 1958. *1913 nien-1952 nien nan-k'ai chih-shu tzu-liao hui-pein* (*A compendium of Nankai Indexes, 1913–1925*). Peking.

Nankai University Economic Research Bureau, 1963. *Ch'i-hsin yang-hui kung-ssu shih-liao* (*Historical Documents on the Ch'i-hsin Cement Company*). Peking.

Northeast China Economic Commission, 1947. *Chih-chi chih-chiang* (*Paper and Pulp*), *Tung-pei ching-chi hsiao ts'ung-shu* (*Economic Handbook series on Manchuria*), No. 13. Shenyang.

Nung-shang-pu (Ministry of Agriculture and Commerce), 1914–24. *Nung-shang t'ung-chi piao* (*Statistical Tables on China's Agriculture and Commerce*), Nos. 1 to 10. Shanghai.

Nung-shang-pu (Ministry of Agriculture and Commerce), 1922. *Ti-ch'i-tz'u nung-shang t'ung-chi piao (Statistical Tables of the Ministry of Agriculture and Commerce)*, No. 7. Peking.

OU PAO-SAN *et al.*, 1947(a). *Chung-kuo kuo-min so-te, 1933 nien (China's National Income, 1933)*. (Institute of Social Sciences, Academia Sinica, Monograph series, No. 25, Vols. I and II.) Shanghai.

OU PAO-SAN, 1947(b). "Chung kuo kuo-min so-te, 1933, hsiu-cheng" ("China's National Income, 1933, Revised"), *She-hui k'o-hsüeh tsa-chih (Social Science Quarterly)*, Vol. 9, No. 2 (December, 1947), pp. 92–153.

P'ENG TSE-YI (Ed.), 1957. *Chung-kuo chin-tai shou-kung-yeh shih tzŭ-liao, 1840–1949 (Source Materials on the Modern History of Chinese Handicrafts)*. Peking.

Shen-pao nien-chien (Shen-pao Yearbook), 1934, 1936. Shanghai.

Shih-yeh-pu (Ministry of Industries), 1934, 1935, 1936. *Chung-kuo ching-chi nien-chien (Chinese Economic Yearbook)*. Shanghai.

Shih-yeh-pu (Ministry of Industries), 1936—. *Shih-yeh-pu yüeh-k'an (Monthly Bulletin of the Ministry of Industries)*. Nanking.

Shih-yeh-pu (Ministry of Industries), 1933—. *Shih-yeh t'ung-chi (Industrial Statistics)*. Nanking.

South Manchuria Railway, 1930. *Manshū ni okeru semento kōgyō to sono jūkyū jōkyō (Supply and Demand Conditions of Cement in Manchuria)*. Dairen.

South Manchuria Railway, 1931. *Manshū no sen'i kōgyō (Manchuria's Textile Industries)*. Dairen.

South Manchuria Railway, 1935, 1936, 1938. *Manshū keizai tōkei nempō (Manchurian Economic Statistics Yearbook)*. Dairen.

South Manchuria Railway, 1938. *Manshū keizai nempō (Manchurian Economic Yearbook)*. Dairen.

South Manchuria Railway, 1938. *Manshū keizai teiyō (Elements of Manchurian Economy)*. Dairen.

South Manchuria Railway, 1942. *Manshū keizai tōkei kihō (Manchurian Economic Statistics Quarterly)*, Nos. 2 and 3. Dairen.

State Statistical Bureau, 1959. *Wei-ta ti shih-nien, (Ten Great Years)*. Peking.

State Statistical Bureau, 1958. *Wo-kuo kang-t'ieh tien-li mei-t'an chi-hsieh fang-chih tsao-chih kung-yeh ti chin-hsi* (*Past and Present Conditions of the Iron and Steel, Electric Power, Coal, Machinery, Textile, and Paper Industries in China*). Peking.

T'AN HSI-HUNG, 1948. *Shih-nien lai chih Chung-kuo ching-chi* (*The Chinese Economy during the Past Ten Years*). 3 Vols. Shanghai.

WANG CH'ENG-CHING, 1947. *Tung-pei chih ching-chi tzū-yuan* (*Economic Resources of Manchuria*). Shanghai.

WANG FOH-SHEN, 1948b. "Hua-pei chan-shih kung-yeh sheng-ch'an chih-shu" ("Indexes of Industrial Production for Wartime North China"), *Ching-chi p'ing-lun* (*Economic Critic*), Vol. 2, No. 14 (January 3, 1948).

WANG TZU-CHIEN and WANG CHEN-CHUNG, 1935. *Ch'i-sheng hua-shang sha-ch'ang tiao-ch'a pao-kao* (*Report of a Survey of Chinese Cotton Mills in Seven Provinces*). Shanghai.

Wu Ch'eng-lo, 1929. *Chin-shih Chung-kuo shih-yeh t'ung-chih* (*History of Modern Industries in China*), Vols. 1 and 2. Shanghai.

YANG CH'ÜAN, 1923. "Wu-shih-nien-lai Chung-kuo chih kung-yeh" ("Chinese Industries in the Past Fifty Years") *in Tsui-chin chih wu-shih nien, Shen-pao-kuan wu-shih chou-nien chi-nien* (*The Past Fifty Years, in Commemoration of the Shen Pao's Golden Jubilee, 1872–1922*). Shanghai.

YANG TA-CHIN, 1938. *Hsien-tai Chung-kuo shih-yeh chih* (*Modern Chinese Industry*), Vols. 1 and 2. Changsha.

YEN CHUNG-P'ING, 1955. *Chung-kuo mien-fang-chih shih-kao* (*A Draft History of Chinese Cotton Spinning and Weaving*). Peking.

YEN CHUNG-P'ING et al. (Eds.), 1955. *Chung-kuo chin-tai ching-chi shih t'ung-chi tzū-liao hsüan-chih* (*Selected Statistics on the Economic History of Modern China*). Peking.

PART II: ENGLISH

BURNS, ARTHUR F., 1934. *Production Trends in the U.S. Since 1879*. New York.

Bureau of Information, 1947. *China Handbook, 1937–1945.* Shanghai.

CHAO KANG, 1965. *The Rate and Pattern of Industrial Growth in Communist China.* Ann Arbor, Michigan.

CHEN HAN-SENG, 1947. *Gung Ho! The Story of the Chinese Cooperatives.* IPR Pamphlet No. 24. New York.

CHENG CHU-YUAN, 1963. *Communist China's Economy, 1949–1962, Structural Changes and Crisis.* South Orange, N.J.

CHENG YU-K'WEI, 1956. *Foreign Trade and Industrial Development of China.* Washington, D.C.

CHIN ROCKWOOD, 1937. *Cotton Mills, Japan's Economic Spearhead in China. A Study in International Competition.* (Unpublished doctoral dissertation, Yale University.)

The China Annual, 1944, 1945. Shanghai.

The China Yearbook, 1926–27. Shanghai.

Chinese Association for the United Nations, 1952. *A Report on Russian Destruction of Our Industries in the North-eastern Provinces.* Taipei.

CRAWCOUR, E. SYDNEY, 1965. "The Tokugawa Heritage," in William W. Lockwood (ed.), *The State and Economic Enterprise in Japan.* Princeton.

ECKSTEIN, ALEXANDER, 1966. *Communist China's Economic Growth and Foreign Trade.* New York.

ECKSTEIN, ALEXANDER, 1958. "Individualism and the Role of the State in Economic Growth," *Economic Development and Cultural Change,* Vol. 6, No. 2 (January, 1958), pp. 81–87.

FABRICANT, SOLOMON, 1940. *The Output of Manufacturing Industries, 1899–1937.* New York.

FAIRBANK, JOHN K., ECKSTEIN, ALEXANDER, and YANG, L. S., 1960. "Economic Change in Early Modern China: An Analytic Framework," *Economic Development and Cultural Change,* Vol. 9, No. 1 (October, 1960), pp. 1–26.

The Far East Year Book, 1941. Tokyo.

FEUERWERKER, ALBERT, 1958. *China's Early Industrialization, Shen Hsuan-huai (1844–1916) and Mandarin Enterprise.* Cambridge, Mass.

FEUERWERKER, ALBERT, 1964. "China's Nineteenth Century Industrialization: The Case of the Hanyehping Coal and Iron Company, Limited," in C. D. Cowan (ed.), *The Economic Development of China and Japan*. London.

FEUERWERKER, ALBERT, 1966 (ed.). *Modern China*. Englewood Cliffs, N.J.

"Flour Industry in Kiangsu," *Chinese Economic Journal* (July, 1933), pp. 32–48.

"Flour Mills In China," 1928. *Chinese Economic Journal* (June, 1928), pp. 533–542.

"Flour Mills in China," 1930. *British Chamber of Commerce Journal*, No. 137 (November, 1930), pp. 323–324.

The Geological Survey of China, 1921–45. *General Statement on the Mining Industry*, Nos. 1 to 7.

GERSCHENKRON, ALEXANDER, 1965. *Economic Backwardness in Historical Perspective*. New York.

GILLIN, DONALD G., 1967. *Warlord: Yen Hsi-shan in Shansi Province, 1911–1949*. Princeton.

Great Britain, Economic Missions, 1931. *Report of the Cotton Mission*. London.

HODGMAN, DONALD R., 1954. *Soviet Industrial Production, 1928–1951*. Cambridge, Mass.

HOU CHI-MING, 1965. *Foreign Investment and Economic Development in China, 1840–1937*. Cambridge, Mass.

HUNG, FRED C., 1958. "Rates and Patterns of Industrial Growth in Modern China." A paper presented to the Tenth Annual Meeting of the Association for Asian Studies, New York City.

Inspection and Commerce, Vol. 6, No. 1 (January, 1935).

Japan-Manchoukuo Year Book, 1934–40. Tokyo.

KUZNETS, SIMON, 1959. *Six Lectures on Economic Growth*. Glencoe, Ill.

KUZNETS, SIMON, 1966. *Modern Economic Growth, Rate, Structure, and Spread*. New Haven and London.

LIU TA-CHUNG, 1946. *China's National Income, 1931–1936*. Washington, D.C.

LIU TA-CHUNG and YEH KUNG-CHIA, 1965. *The Economy of the Chinese Mainland: National Income and Economic Development, 1933–1959.* Princeton.

LOCKWOOD, WILLIAM W., 1954. *The Economic Development of Japan: Growth and Structural Change, 1868–1938.* Princeton.

LOCKWOOD, WILLIAM W., 1965. "Prospectus and Summary," in W. W. Lockwood (ed.), *The State and Economic Enterprise in Japan.* Princeton.

LU CH'UNG-TAI,1963. "An Interim Understanding of the Concept of Handicraft as the Term is Used in Communist China." Unpublished paper prepared for the First Research Conference of the Social Science Research Council Committee on the Economy of China, Berkeley.

The Manchoukuo Year Book, 1931–34. Tokyo.

ODELL, RALPH M., 1916. *Cotton Goods in China.* Washington, D.C.

The Orient Year Book, 1942. Tokyo

OU PAO-SAN, 1948. *Capital Formation and Consumers' Outlay in China.* (Unpublished doctoral dissertation, Harvard University.)

PAAUW, DOUGLAS S., 1957. "The Kuomintang and Economic Stagnation, 1928–37," *Journal of Asian Studies,* Vol. 16, No. 2 (February, 1957), pp. 213–220.

PAULEY, EDWIN S., 1946. *A Report on Japanese Assets in Manchuria to the President of the United States.* Washington. D.C.

PEARSE, ARNO, 1927. *Cotton Industry of Japan and China.* Manchester.

PERKINS, DWIGHT H., 1966. *Market Control and Planning in Communist China.* Cambridge, Mass.

PERKINS, DWIGHT H., 1967. "Government as an Obstacle to Industrialization: The Case of Nineteenth-Century China," *Journal of Economic History,* Vol. 27, No. 4 (December, 1967), pp. 478–492.

PESEK, BORIS P., 1961. "Economic Growth and Its Measurement," *Economic Development and Cultural Change*, Vol. 9, No. 3 (April, 1961), pp. 295–315.

SUN KUNGTU C. (assisted by Ralph W. Huenemann), 1969. *The Economic Development of Manchuria in the First Half of the Twentieth Century*. Cambridge, Mass.

United Nations, 1949. *Economic Survey of Asia and the Far East*. New York.

United Nations, 1961. *Index Numbers of Industrial Production*. New York.

U.S., Board of Governors, Federal Reserve System, 1960. *Industrial Production, 1959 Revision*. Washington, D.C.

U.S. Department of Interior, Bureau of Mines, 1960. *Mineral Trade Notes*, Supplement No. 59 to Vol. 50, No. 3. Washington, D.C.

U.S. War Trade Board, 1919. *Economic Resources of China*. Washington, D.C.

WANG FOH-SHEN, 1948a. *China's Industrial Production, 1931–1946*. Nanking.

WOLF, H. M., 1934. "The Tobacco Industry in China," *Chinese Economic Journal*, Vol. 14 (January, 1934), pp. 90–104.

WU YUAN-LI, 1956. *An Economic Survey of Communist China*. New York.

WU YUAN-LI, 1965. *The Economy of Communist China*. New York.

YEH KUNG-CHIA, 1964. *Capital Formation in Mainland China: 1931–36 and 1952–57*. (Unpublished doctoral dissertation, Columbia University.)

YIN HELEN and YIN YI-CH'ANG, 1960. *Economic Statistics of Mainland China (1949–1957)*. Cambridge, Mass.

Index